THE
VIOLATED
VISION

THE
VIOLATED
VISION

*The Rape of
Canada's North*

James Woodford

McClelland and Stewart Limited
TORONTO/MONTREAL

The Canadian Publishers
McClelland and Stewart Limited
25 Hollinger Road, Toronto 374

PRINTED AND BOUND IN CANADA

To Beth and Lynn
Two reasons to care

contents

INTRODUCTION

The Arctic may be rich in resources, but it is biologically poor. Low temperatures, sparse soils and other factors have created ecological systems unlike any other on earth. They pose serious and special problems both for man and nature.

Ecologists warn that disruption of northern natural systems may have widespread, even world-wide, effects–the extent of which is just beginning to be realized. For example, the Arctic may control the weather over much of the northern hemisphere. Interference with the arctic ice-pack, which might be caused by a major oil spill or well blow-out, could have disastrous results.

Until recently, nature was the major force shaping the face of the north. Now it is man and his machines. Latter-day robber barons, aided, abetted and encouraged by prodigal politicians and obsequious bureaucrats, are staging an unprecedented industrial invasion–using twentieth-century technology guided by nineteenth-century philosophy.

Despite growing public concern for the environment, it appears that government measures to protect and preserve Canada's Arctic are being delayed, perhaps in the hope that a major discovery would trigger a massive exploration/exploitation "boom" and the Gross National Greed would overwhelm environmental considerations and concerns.

While no government can proclaim polar bears or pingos, the Government of Canada seems unable to proclaim legislation to protect the environment of the third of Canada north of the sixtieth parallel.

The Arctic Waters Pollution Prevention Act and the Northern Inland Waters Act received royal assent on June 26, 1970. The last paragraph of both reads, "This Act shall come into force on a day to be fixed by proclamation." As this is being written, over a year and a half has passed and neither Act has been proclaimed. Territorial Land Use Regulations, first promised in 1969, are still under review, and an Act to regulate northern mineral exploration and mining was withdrawn recently for further study. Arctic Canada is still virtually unprotected.

Over the years there have been several northern "booms"– the search for whales, the gold seekers, and the "radar rush." Recently John Diefenbaker rekindled interest in the Arctic with his vision of "a new Canada. A Canada of the North."

The vision, Peter C. Newman wrote ruefully, soon became a mirage. Now it threatens to become a nightmare. Clearly industry, government, science, and the public were not prepared for the current rush for resources.

As there is no non-renewable resource found in the Arctic which is in short supply in Canada, we should seriously question present policies and programs of northern development. What are the goals of northern development? Who shall benefit from this? Are the interests of the Indians and Eskimos being looked after? Should there be a halt to industrial activity in the Arctic until ecology catches up with technology?

At present the north is being lost, but it is not too late to save it if we recognize that down north it is man, not nature, that must be managed.

James Woodford.

"Government is an uncertain watch-dog, alternately barking and licking its chops."

Robert B. Weeden

CHAPTER I / *Damn the Ecology–Full Speed Ahead!*

A pillar of fire, stretching 250 feet skyward, lit up the Land of the Midnight Sun for ninety-one days. This 25-storey flare was fuelled by over nine billion cubic feet of natural gas, burning at an estimated rate of a hundred million cubic feet per day.

Panarctic Oil's wildcat well on King Christian Island, only 850 miles from the North Pole, blew out of control on October 25, 1970. The initial eruption of sand, gas, water and rock and the fire that followed destroyed a $1 million drill rig; miraculously, none of the crew were killed or suffered permanent injury. The flames created a "deafening roar" and provided ample light, in the 24-hour darkness, for the wild well killing operations. Numerous small fires, resulting from gas escaping from fissures, created a "ring of fire" up to seven hundred feet from the well hole.

But King Christian wasn't the first Panarctic well to blow wild.

Panarctic's first Arctic Islands well was spudded at Drake Point on Melville Island on April 19, 1969. Drake Point L-67 blew out of control on July 13, 1969, spewing up a mixture of natural gas and water. An American expert, brought in to try and shut off the well, reported that a "routine approach" was not feasible because of impossible working conditions on and around the drilling rig. In late July, L-67 was shut off–only to blow out again on August 30.

"The gas-water mixture emission from L-67 rapidly built a huge ice cone (estimated to be 125 feet high) in the cold temperatures . . ."[1] reported "Bev" Parmenter, Exploration Editor of *Oilweek*.

Two hundred and sixty-eight days later, on May 25, 1970, *Oilweek* carried the following late news item: "A relief well drilled by Panarctic Oils Limited to shut off its wild gas well at Drake Point . . . may have accomplished part of its mission. Company officials report that the gas flow from the lower sands is now apparently shut off. . . . However, water continues to flow. . . ."[2] On July 20, 1970, *Oilweek* reported that: "A second relief well will be spudded shortly by Panarctic Oils aimed at sealing off the gas-laden formation water still blowing from the original Drake Point wildcat. . . ."[3]

It was now over a year since L-67 first blew out of control, emitting gas at the rate, roughly estimated by a government conservation engineer, of about three million cubic feet per day. Panarctic's Exploration Manager, G. P. Crombie, suggests that if we assume a liberal ten million cubic feet per day the total volume released up to May 20, 1970, would be 2.72 billion cubic feet of gas–"little more than a half day's sales from all Canadian wells"[4]–but worth over $2 million delivered to Toronto.

The wild well on King Christian had the added problem of fire. A new drill rig was flown in by Hercules aircraft. After preliminary drilling, a relief hole was started, about 700 feet away, set at a 26-degree angle to intersect with the wild well. Sea water, carried to the site through two nine-inch lines, laid one-and-one-half miles from the well to the ocean, was pumped down the relief hole, at the rate of 4,100 gallons per minute, for twelve hours.

At first, the gas continued to burn and steam sizzled high into the sky. Chunks of formation rock, broken off by the injected water, were hurled hazardously through the air.

After about ten hours the fire finally appeared to be out. As a precaution, water was pumped in for another two hours. Injection was then switched to mud, which was circulated down the relief hole and up the original well to make sure the fire was dead. Then 1,500 sacks of cement were pumped down the relief hole. Finally, ninety-one days later, the wild well was plugged, at a cost of nearly $2 million.

Panarctic's prophets of panacea say there was no environmental damage caused by the King Christian wild well. Perhaps they are right. But even inspecting the area must have been difficult, if not impossible, given the twenty-four-hour darkness at that time of year. Of greater importance is the fact that the site had not been examined by ecologists and other scientists, either before or after drilling began and the well blew out of control. This creates a classic credibility gap—or chasm.

If either of these blow-outs "had been oil instead of gas, Canada would at this very moment be deeply embroiled in the most massive case of oil pollution in her history," warned Dr. Richard E. Warner, in a report prepared under contract for the Canadian Wildlife Service. "And since the Government [of Canada] owns 45 per cent of the stock of Panarctic Oils Limited, the Government may find itself in the most unenviable position of becoming a major polluter of the environment while simultaneously trying to curb pollution by others."[5]

Panarctic's operations are little credit to a government publicly committed to preserving "the peculiar ecological balance in the . . . Canadian Arctic." The myopic Minister of Northern Development, Jean Chrétien, told a meeting of Texas oilmen that "one discovery for every four wells drilled is not a bad ratio . . . ."[6] One *blow-out* for every four wells drilled is not a good ratio. It is an appallingly bad safety record, unprecedented in the history of oil/gas exploration anywhere in the world.

Because of the government's involvement and investment ($34.2 million to date) Panarctic should be expected to set high standards for the oil/gas industry, when operating in the fragile ecological conditions found over much of the Arctic. This has not been the case.

Panarctic has been "island-hopping" in what amounts to a "high-grade" program of wildcat wells in frantic attempts to discover oil and/or natural gas. Their program seems a rather unsystematic one, based as much on drilling wells on lands held under permit by other companies–and in which Panarctic can earn an interest if it attempts a certain number of wells on this acreage–as it is on geological-geophysical data.

None of Panarctic's well sites have been examined, before beginning drilling, by a multi-disciplinary team of ecologists, biologists, botanists and other scientists, to gather "baseline" data on the area and to determine if the sites were of special scientific value or harboured rare or endangered plants or animals. For example, it would be disastrous to drill a well on a polar bear denning area or a caribou calving ground. Apparently, there are no ecologists either on Panarctic's staff or retained as consultants.

M. P. Martial Asselin told the House of Commons that "on Melville Island, where Panarctic Oils Limited is conducting operations there are thousands of oil drums scattered about the island. The delicate wildlife of the island has already fallen victim to the machinery in use there."[7] Drake Point, scene of a wild well blow-out, has been classified by the Canadian Wildlife Service as an "important" wildlife area "necessary to the maintenance or survival of wildlife populations."

The Commons Standing Committee on Indian Affairs and Northern Development (SCIAND) was highly critical of Panarctic and the Government's oil pollution disaster group, in a report which pointed "to a serious lack of knowledge, worldwide, as to the destructive effects of hydrocarbon pollution in Arctic waters."[8] The government's oil pollution disaster group "did not bother to send a representative north to investigate the extent of oil pollution resulting from the [Panarctic] barge sinking."[9] The SCIAND was highly critical of Panarctic's moving supplies by barge to its bases on the Arctic Islands.

Mr. Chrétien told the House of Commons that the original objectives of Panarctic were stimulation of oil and gas exploration in Canada's Arctic Islands, maintenance of Canadian ownership and control of oil and gas rights over a large sector of this potentially rich oil basin, development of a Canadian technology suitable to northern terrain and climate, and creation of employment opportunities for northern residents.

The late J. C. Sproule, the man credited with first proposing the Panarctic concept, wrote: "The tempo of interest in the [Arctic] islands by the oil industry reached a high peak between 1960 and 1963 when over 50 million acres were filed on, mainly by individuals and independent oil companies. . . . Since much of this acreage had been taken up by speculators . . . interest began to wane. . . . Most of this acreage would have reverted to the Crown and returned to the 'deepfreeze' at this time had not Panarctic been formed. . . ."[10] From a conservation point of view this would have been most desirable, but in the early sixties there was little concern for the arctic environment.

Undoubtedly, Panarctic, and perhaps more importantly, the massive oil find at Prudhoe Bay in Alaska, have stimulated exploration and activity in northern Canada by many of the major oil companies. However, since Panarctic was established in December 1967, private industry has, until quite recently, concentrated most of its efforts on the northern mainland, especially the Mackenzie Delta region, leaving the "greater risk— higher cost" Arctic Archipelago wildcat well drilling to Panarctic. This paid off with Imperial Oil Limited's oil find at Atkinson Point, north-east of Inuvik, on January 15, 1970, and a smaller oil strike in the Eagle Plains area by Western Minerals.

As the federal government already controls all the natural

resources except game north of the sixtieth parallel, it is not clear just how Panarctic's operations will add to this control —unless the Government maintains its 45 per cent interest through to production and distribution. Former Panarctic President John M. Taylor was quoted in the *Globe and Mail* as saying that he is certain that the government role should be in the exploration phase of the venture and not extended into the "downstream" operations if oil and gas are found in commercial quantities. Besides, Panarctic controls less than ten per cent of the total Arctic acreage under permit or lease. Panarctic was to have drilled nineteen wells in a program that would have earned it an eighty per cent interest in any finds on about 44 million acres. Now, the program has been reduced to fourteen wells and Panarctic has farmed out some of its exploratory rights to various other companies—all of them *foreign-owned*. Thus, the public interest in lands over which the public had, until recently, outright control, has been reduced.

At the January 1970 session of the Council of the Northwest Territories, Councillor Duncan Pryde revealed that although the government had invested nine million dollars in the Panarctic venture, only six Eskimos and no other territorial residents had been employed. In answer to a question in the House of Commons, Northern Development Parliamentary Secretary Russell C. Honey reported that only four Eskimos were employed by Panarctic's contractors as labourers at the rate of $1.75 per hour—less than half the going rate in Toronto.

Another important consideration is: how much control does the government actually have over Panarctic's operations? Former President Taylor says: "they leave the operation to us and there is no interference." Although the government has a 45 per cent interest in Panarctic, they have only four directors on Panarctic's Board. The government directors are senior civil servants (deputy minister rank), rather than Members of Parliament. Considering the large investment of public funds,

16

should there not be a majority of government-appointed directors, including, perhaps, some Members of Parliament?

"We need more analysis and less propaganda about projects like Panarctic," suggests Professor Jim Lotz.[11] Surely it is time for a hard-nosed, public look at Panarctic's operations and objectives, by a Royal Commission, a Parliamentary Committee, or a special task force. There are many questions which, in the public interest, should be answered:

*Why was the Drake Point wildcat well allowed to blow out of control for over a year?

*Why are so few Eskimos, Indians, and Métis employed by Panarctic?

*Is Panarctic's program based on adequate geological-geophysical data?

*Why does the government, which owns a 45 per cent interest, have only four seats on Panarctic's board of directors?

*Why have there been no ecological studies of drilling sites?

*Why does the government refuse to slow down the pace of arctic oil exploration when Panarctic's operations show clearly that technology is inadequate to cope with arctic conditions?

*Why has the government not committed itself beyond the exploration stage?

*Should the government be in the oil business?

*If it is, who then regulates the regulators?

One of the most perplexing questions is how, if at all, has the government's interest in Panarctic affected its programs to protect and preserve the environment north of the sixtieth parallel. For example, if a private company (rather than Panarctic) had a well blow out of control would the government have acted differently? If the government were not in the oil business would it have enacted and enforced its (as of November 1971) still nebulous Northern Land Use Regulations?

17

In 1969, the Department of Indian Affairs and Northern Development (DIAND) began drafting Northern Land Use Regulations (NLUR). DIAND Minister Chrétien explained that the basic concept is that "all resource exploration and development, using power equipment, conducted on public land in the far North will be permitted only under the authority of a Land-Use permit . . . to reduce or eliminate damage to the environment and to provide for the protection of the landscape in certain areas."[12]

Chrétien told the Canadian Institute of Forestry in October of 1969 that "what will appear finally in the form of regulations will really be a code of behaviour which has been reached between industry and government. . . ." A questionable arrangement, to say the least, especially in view of the Minister's remark, "I am acutely aware of the economic realities of operating in the North and will ensure that we do not go to extremes."[13]

Later that month, the concept of NLUR (the Regulations themselves remained secret) was discussed by delegates at the World Tundra Conference in Edmonton. Considerable concern was expressed that the announced make-up of the committee drafting the Regulations did not include a broad enough spectrum of interests and expertise—especially in the ecology-conservation sector. This concern was reflected in a resolution, passed unanimously on October 17, 1969, which reads, in part:

> . . . the importance of the proposed land-use regulations and their technical complexity require that they receive the broadest scrutiny of those who have knowledge and experience to offer. Therefore, the Department of Indian Affairs and Northern Development should take advantage of this knowledge and experience by broadly circulating the proposed land-use regulations and by inviting written submissions and possibly public hearings.[14]

Subsequently, three more carefully selected conservationists were added to the NLUR Advisory Committee. But public hearings on the draft Regulations have not been held and no national or provincial conservation association has been invited to submit briefs or proposals. Not even the Commons Standing Committee on Indian Affairs and Northern Development has been allowed to examine the draft of regulations that will govern land use in an area larger than all but fourteen of the world's countries.

The April 6, 1970 issue of *Oilweek* reported that an advisory committee on northern land use, including representatives of industry and conservation associations, had been established by DIAND. This committee had agreed to a set of Northern Land Use Regulations, and according to Mr. Chrétien most industries surveyed by his department had voluntarily agreed to the new rules.

How could industry agree to the land use regulations unless they had an opportunity to examine them? If industry did see the draft regulations, why are members of Parliament denied the same opportunity? Is it really possible that a Minister of the Crown could be so naive as to believe that private enterprise would "police" itself—considering the multi-billion dollar stakes in the Arctic?

Corporate social responsibility is a phrase often heard these days. How far does this responsibility go in the realm of private versus public good? The president of the Independent Petroleum Association of Canada, Alastair H. Ross, warned the government to ". . . go easy on its new land regulations . . . to avoid scaring off companies. . . ."[15] And W. O. Twaits, chairman of Imperial Oil's board of directors, believes that the Arctic and other frontier areas "cannot carry unduly heavy burdens of regulation. . . ."[16] So much for corporate social responsibility and the notion that private oil companies will regulate themselves.

A letter to the editor in *Oilweek* (May 18, 1970) under the headline "Reservations re Conservation" commented on the April 6 report as follows:

... we object to this statement [as quoted above] as untrue insofar as it says the conservation representatives have agreed to the new Land Use Regulations. We are expressly on record with the Department as reserving our approval because in the course of deliberation of the advisory committee, *the Department indicated a viewpoint on important matters we found unacceptable.* In a broad way, without going into detail, these objections centered around the facts that *the land use operations of the mining industry would largely be excepted from the regulations* and therefore continue to be unregulated as in the past, and that *the regulations would lack effective enforcement and sanctions.*[17] [Emphasis added.]

The letter was signed by NLUR Advisory Committee members A. R. Thompson (Professor of Law, University of British Columbia), Gavin Henderson (Executive Director, National and Provincial Parks Association), Dr. John Lambert (Professor of Botany, Carleton University), John Lammers (President, Yukon Conservation Society), Richard C. Passmore (Executive Director, Canadian Wildlife Federation) and Dr. W. Pruitt (Professor of Biology, University of Manitoba).

Little wonder that the Regulations have been a closely guarded secret! Without effective enforcement and penalties the Regulations would at best be of doubtful value in protecting the northern environment and at worst tend to deceive the public, who would be unaware of what was really happening.

Evidently the full NLUR Advisory Committee met only once or twice and virtually none of the recommendations made by the conservation representatives were added to the draft Regulations.

A leading Canadian conservationist, Douglas H. Pimlott, stated that "subsequently three members of the committee were critical of developments and *none* of the three was invited to take part in a task force that recently visited some sites in the western Arctic."[18]

This Task Force on Conservation was part of a "sweeping development, conservation program for the North" unveiled by Mr. Chrétien in Winnipeg on May 4, 1970, at the Sixth Annual Meeting of the Canadian Transportation Research Forum.

The task force, composed of three scientists, two conservationists, three oil company employees and two civil servants, visited the Mackenzie Delta region from May 11 to 16, 1970. The terms of reference were outlined by A. D. Hunt (Assistant Deputy-Minister, Northern Development) as follows:

1. Investigate and describe current environmental problems associated with resource development operations in the Mackenzie Delta region.
2. Make recommendations on land use or other stipulations that could be incorporated immediately into the Department of Indian Affairs and Northern Development's Land Use Regulations and which would further reduce damage to the environment.
3. Make recommendations and establish priorities on problems for which longer term research is required under the Department of Indian Affairs and Northern Development's Arctic Land Use Research Program (ALUR).
4. Make a written report on the above matters to the Minister of Indian Affairs and Northern Development.[19]

All this in the space of five days. Only two days were spent in the field inspecting drilling sites, seismic operations and environmental damage, and one of these days was spent in an aircraft "generously" provided by Imperial Oil Limited.

A DIAND "communiqué" dated June 29, 1970, announced that "the group reported some damage to the environment but tentatively concluded it was minimal."[20] The actual report of the task force qualified the above as follows: ". . . [the] duration of the trip, without further observation, precludes the task force from testing the thesis that irreparable environmental damage may be occurring."[21]

And while the DIAND communiqué concludes that "the task force stated that the timing of the trip was such that a follow-up inspection trip will be necessary this summer . . . ,"[22] the task force report bluntly concluded:

> The timing and duration of the trip, as is well recognized by all concerned, were entirely inappropriate. In early May, industrial exploration activities were at their lowest level; winter work had stopped, with a few exceptions and summer work had not started. Also, the climatic conditions of the time of year (maximum snow cover and frozen ground) precluded any serious, critical examination of surface conditions.[23]

The task force further qualified its report with the following:

1. The group was not furnished with documentation on the past and present industrial activities in the region, and on the extent and nature of research and surveys by government and other agencies.
2. The group lacked any specific information on the Land Use Regulations which are being formulated currently, and this hampered seriously the effectiveness and relevance of any discussion and recommendations in this regard.[24]

Contrast this with another group that the Minister of Northern Development invited to tour the Arctic in August of 1968. They received detailed background material, including maps, photographs, and flight log, in a lavish, specially prepared book. They travelled in a chartered Pacific Western Airlines DC-6B. This party was made up of oil and mining company executives, politicians and bureaucrats.

"It is a travesty on the use of the term to call a two-day visit to the Arctic a task force,"[25] charges ecologist Dr. Douglas H. Pimlott of the University of Toronto and senior author of a recent (1970) Report to the Privy Council on Fisheries and Wildlife Research in Canada. Pimlott maintains that "If a task force is to be more than a token effort it should be conducted for at least two and a half months (June 15 to September 1) and it should be made up of at least a dozen people who range over a variety of disciplines; anything less is tokenism."[26]

One of the members of the task force, Richard C. Passmore, revealed in the *Canadian Wildlife Federation Newsletter* (Spring 1970) that the CWF, about mid-February, 1970, "suggested that the Task Force should make its initial field inspection while winter seismic, drilling and transportation operations could still be observed, to be followed by a longer and more detailed inspection trip to be made during the summer months."[27] Was the delay due to political procrastination, bureaucratic bungling, or both? Or is it possible that the Government does not really want a searching, scientific look at the threats and damage, actual and potential, to the arctic environment which may result from industrial activity?

The world watched in awe when in September, 1969, the State of Alaska, following a "billion barrel plus" oil discovery at Prudhoe Bay, received almost a million dollars for leases on just 800 square miles, adjoining the discovery wells. Imperial Oil's Atkinson Point oil find should have triggered one of the biggest land sales in Canada's history. But there wasn't any billion dollar bonanza for the people of Canada. For they were dealt out of this first opportunity to recoup some of their three quarters of a billion dollar investment in the north by legislation which petroleum lawyer A. R. Thompson, co-author of the authoritative *Canadian Oil and Gas* termed ". . . foolish give-aways in the eagerness to exploit Arctic oil for political and prestige purposes."[28]

Thompson was referring to Oil and Gas Land Order No. 1-1961, proclaimed in the Diefenbaker days and continued under the Pearson and until recently, the Trudeau administrations. Order 1-1961 deals with the granting of oil and gas permits and leases. It was somewhat unique in that the regulations "do not, as provincial legislation does, include a public reserve and bonus bid system as a principal measure for providing revenue, the Federal legislation does not, as provincial legislation does, permit a periodic revision of royalty rates under existing leases to ensure that the public interest continues to receive its fair share of production revenue."[29]

The regulations contained such incentive features as double credits for deep wildcat wells, special renewal provisions, unusually liberal grouping provisions, no rental and low initial royalties, establishment of work credit accounts whenever companies required them, allowance of off-permit work and research to earn permits, and additional allowance of 12.5 per cent to permit expenditures to cover administration costs.

What are the implications of this loss of potential revenue? First, the Canadian taxpayer might have been relieved of much of the burden of supporting government programs and "private" development incentive schemes in the north; second, it might have provided funds to settle long outstanding land claims of the original peoples; third, it might have ensured funding for ecological, engineering, and other desperately needed research; and fourth, it might have furnished the monies necessary to adequately enforce land use regulations and a conservation program worthy of the name.

On April 15, 1970, without warning and prior consultation with industry, Oil and Gas Land Order No. 1-1961 was revoked by joint order of Northern Development Minister Chrétien and Energy Minister Greene. Naturally, the petroleum people were upset and unhappy. The Canadian Petroleum Association's executive director, David B. Furlong, cited the revoking of Land Order 1-1961 as "akin to a landlord dumping his tenant's furniture on the sidewalk as a prelude to discussing a change in the rent."[30]

Gene E. Roark, past-president of the Independent Petroleum Association of Canada, complained that "every time Ottawa makes an announcement that changes prevailing rules of the game, its effects on investor circles are widespread."[31] And oil writer Carl O. Nickle wondered: "Does the killing of the 1961 Order by government without consultation with industry mark a new trend in a nation whose honour has kept Canada in sharp contrast to certain banana republics and Asian-African oil states?"[32]

"The oil industry," complained CPA's Furlong, "has invested about $440 million in exploration of these regions making bids and commitments on the basis of one set of rules and regulations, only to have them unilaterally and suddenly changed without prior consultation or warning."[33]

But before you weep for Shell or Gulf or Imperial, consider what former Finance Minister Walter Gordon wrote in *A Choice for Canada*: ". . . the petroleum industry . . . pays very little tax compared with other industries; it benefits from depletion allowances as well as capital-cost allowances; and the integrated oil companies may offset their development and exploration expenditures against profits earned on distribution."[34] In other words, if the capital wasn't spent on exploration it might have been paid as taxes.

By revoking Land Order 1-1961 the government now has the opportunity to replace it with an order incorporating a public reserve and bonus bid system and a revised schedule of royalty rates. But will the new order apply to future holdings only? Panarctic's vice-president, John M. Godfrey, thinks that it will, and that present permit holdings will continue under existing regulations, although "the Government will be less generous in granting discretionary provisions than in the past."[35]

This is another case in which it is clearly in the public interest for public hearings to he held to allow discussion and suggestions from all interested parties. Copies of new draft regulations should be widely circulated, as the Benson White Paper on Taxation has been.

The Chrétien-Greene action may have caused some uncertainty in financial circles–but a billion barrel discovery would soon change that. It is important to keep in mind that when this Order was revoked (and at the time of writing) there had been only one oil and two gas finds in Canada north of the Arctic

Circle, and there are still as yet no proven reserves to make production economic. But if the government acts in the public interest in drawing up the order to replace 1-1961, and includes the public bonus feature, it could be in the position to offer considerable acreage for public auction, when and if the next discovery occurs. From a conservation point of view, a cooling-off of the oil and gas play would be most desirable. The government is clearly not prepared for this northern industrial invasion –which it invited.

In a flurry of flag waving, the House of Commons pushed through Bill C-202–the Arctic Waters Pollution Prevention Act –without seriously questioning its intent or content with respect to arctic ecology and pollution prevention. The vote on second reading was yeas, 198; nays, nil. Debate on this bill, which Prime Minister Trudeau called "the most important measure taken by his government," takes up only 59 pages of *House of Commons Debates*. About the same time an amendment to the Criminal Code respecting hate literature was before the House: debate took up 139 pages.

Bill C-202 was evidently enacted to give the government authority to prevent pollution of the waters in the Arctic, but unfortunately it has been interpreted, rightly or wrongly, as a means of asserting Canada's sovereignty over the Arctic Islands. The area to be protected is carefully detailed and delineated, with greater precision than previously.

Curiously, the thing that is to be prevented, or at least controlled–pollution–is not defined or explained. Evidently pollution is to be prevented by controlling the discharge of waste into arctic waters. Waste is defined (Sec. 2.h.1.) as

> any substance that, if added to any waters, would degrade or alter or form part of a process of degradation of the quality of those waters to an extent that is detrimental to their use by man or by any animal, fish or plant that is useful to man.[36]

This concept of usefulness to man is, as the late Rachel

Carson wrote in *Silent Spring,* "born of the neanderthal age of biology and philosophy, when it was supposed that nature exists for the convenience of man."[37] The authors of Bill C-202 did not understand the basic principles and concepts of ecology.

As it stands the Arctic Waters Pollution Prevention Act is a lawyer's dream. Arguments with respect to what is useful to man could go on for years. Is the polar bear of use? Is the plankton in the Arctic Ocean of use? What of the frozen seas themselves?

Who shall make these value judgements? Politicians . . . bureaucrats . . . lawyers . . . scientists . . . you or I? Who among us is to say, given man's present incomplete knowledge of arctic ecology, that this animal or that plant is of no use to man–and therefore, that it matters little (if at all) if it is destroyed? It's rather chilling when one realizes that if man were to inadvertent-ly destroy any one of the half dozen types of bacteria involved in the nitrogen cycle, life on earth might end. The least of the arctic life forms might prove to be the most important.

If the definition of waste in Bill C-202 finished after the phrase "the quality of those waters" it would make sense ecolo-gically and be much easier to enforce–if the government had the will and the wish to do it.

Another very disturbing instance of a lack of ecological un-derstanding is the announcement by Northern Development Minister Chrétien that "companies wishing to use land will . . . pay fees at a standard rate per acre of land affected in the course of their operations."[38]

What price the barren lands? What fees will cover rehabilitat-ing the tundra? Can fees, no matter how high, compensate for irreversible environmental damage? Chrétien admitted that "we lack a good deal of information and data relating to the short and long term effects of man-made disturbance on the northern environment."[39] How then, at this point in time, can any mean-ingful measurement in dollars and cents (if this premise of "dollars for damage" is accepted) be made of the effects of environmental disturbance and degradation? One thing is known: it takes the northern environment much longer to "heal" itself than those of more temperate regions. Any fees should only be regarded as down-payments, because the "costs of rehabilitation and restoration" might be spread over as much as a century. Another important dimension is the possible loss of revenue if damaged lands had been used for other purposes, such as outdoor recreation.

Recent actions and activities of Chrétien and his senior bureaucrats give the impression that, despite a flow of rheumy rhetoric claiming concern for the northern environment, they are still committed to a "boomer-booster" approach to northern development. Conservation is fine, but why don't you worry about pollution problems in the south and let us get on with our growth in the north!

As Richard Passmore reveals in *Wildlife News* (Spring, 1970): "The Canadian Wildlife Federation first expressed its concern to the Department of Indian Affairs and Northern Development some two and one-half years ago, but it became increasingly evident that senior staff of that department were so busy fostering development of the non-renewable resources of the north that there was little likelihood they would broaden their perspective to include conservation of its renewable natural resources."[40]

The most flagrant example of the government's and DIAND's ambiguous attitude to conservation north of 60 is the case of Panarctic's wild wells. Is it not reasonable to assume that if they were really sincere about protecting the northern environment they would have stopped drilling operations in the Arctic until technology came up with new techniques to virtually eliminate the possibility of "blow-outs" like those described earlier? The government's reaction was to praise the wild wells as great discoveries and to invest another $24 million in Panarctic.

If Canada is going to play the Trudeau game of preserving the Arctic's "peculiar ecological balance" the rules must be

28

nature's, not man's. Until this is clearly recognized, and the government begins to legislate and regulate on the basis of ecological reality, we will be faced with the situation described by ecologist Paul Erhlich: "It is the top of the ninth inning. Man, always a threat at the plate, has been hitting Nature hard. It is important to remember, however, that Nature bats last."[41]

Polemics and public relations will not preserve polar bears and pingos, caribou and cladonia, barren lands and belugas. Government is indeed an uncertain watchdog. For example:

1. After two years the Northern Land Use Regulations are not law. Even when they are finally proclaimed the regulations are to be enforced by engineers, *not* ecologists.

2. Regulations still have not been written (November 1971) for the Arctic Waters Pollution Prevention Act and the Northern Inland Waters Act. Without such regulations the Acts are simply "paper legislation."

3. Under the British North America Act, the provinces have jurisdiction over most of Canada's natural resources. The land north of the sixtieth parallel is the only region over which the federal government has complete control of the natural resources. Despite this, the new Department of the Environment will have little control over pollution and other environmental problems in the north. All the Acts dealing with northern conservation are to remain with the Department of Indian Affairs and Northern Development.

Remember, when threatened the beaver doesn't bite. It slaps its tail on the water, which makes a big noise. Then it hides. It will take a revolution in policies, programs and personnel if the north is to be saved from the environmental disturbance, degradation and destruction suffered by the south.

"Tundra has long been one of the few remaining areas in this world which man could ponder or disregard at his leisure."

P. L. Johnson

Arctic plants, ecosystems
and strategies

CHAPTER 2 / *The Tundra World*

Polar parameters are paradoxical. The tundra world is bleak,
yet hauntingly beautiful; frozen, yet extremely fragile.

Down north, the broad belt of boreal forest that covers half
of Canada dissolves into treeless tundra. It is popularly regarded as a vast wasteland (the "cold desert", the "barren
grounds"), but explorer Stephanson called it the "friendly
Arctic," and naturalist Thompson-Seton described in vivid detail the "arctic prairies."

For most of the year it is strikingly inhospitable to life. Plants
lie dormant; most animals take temporary leave. Of all the
arctic mammals, only the ground squirrel truly hibernates. During the long northern night, polar bears and arctic foxes roam
the sea-ice; muskoxen forage by starlight. And of the birds, only
the snowy owl, the raven, and the ptarmigan regularly remain.

Arctic spring comes with a rush. Almost overnight the life-
support systems of the torpid tundra are re-activated by the
returning sun. Long before the snows have vanished the first
flowers appear. The landscape becomes a mosaic of mossy
mounds, rocky outcroppings, ponds and marshy grasslands.

Countless millions of seabirds, shorebirds, and waterfowl surge north to nest.

Polar environmental parameters include such factors as high latitude, long winters, short cool summers, low precipitation, frozen sea and lakes, permafrost, and the absence of trees.

While the absence of trees is most striking, permafrost is the dominant physical feature. Permafrost, or perenially frozen ground, is defined as "the thermal condition of earth materials such as soil and rock when their temperature remains below 32 degrees Fahrenheit continuously for a number of years." The minimum limits for permafrost are from one winter, through a summer, and into the next winter. Permafrost is not "permanently frozen." Changes in terrain and climate may cause it to thaw and disappear. Permafrost may range from a few inches to hundreds of feet thick. At Winter Harbour on Melville Island, the depth is 1,500 feet.

The southern limit of continuous permafrost includes the north-western tip of Quebec, a coastal corridor along Hudson Bay, then diagonally to just north of Great Slave and Great Bear Lakes and westward south of Old Crow in the Yukon. This coincides roughly with the mean annual air isotherm of −1 degree Centigrade (30.2° F). With minor variations, this is the "tree-line"–the "divide" between boreal forest and barren grounds.

Permafrost affects one-fifth of the land area of the Northern Hemisphere. It has profound effects on vegetation, especially tree and shrub-like growth.

One of the most direct effects of permafrost is to "chill" the soil, thus retarding plant growth. On the other hand, vegetation may chill the soil by shielding it from incoming heat. The total annual precipitation (snow, rain) is so small over much of the Arctic, that if it were not for the permafrost providing a frozen barrier just below the surface, thus preventing surface water from sinking beyond the reach of plant roots, much of the Arctic would be a lifeless desert. In spite of a seemingly great excess of water, some of the soil is considered to be "dry," for in low temperatures plants have difficulty in taking up moisture.

The active layer in permafrost regions is quite thin, and minerals in this layer may be used up. Because the material below is frozen, no replacement is possible from the store below. As mentioned earlier, permafrost is not permanent; thawing and heaving may occur, producing such things as polygons, mounds, landslides, and the "drunken forest" effect.

Permafrost has profound effects on the activity of soil micro-organisms, so vital to plant growth. Decay of plant and animal matter, due to the slowing of bacterial action, takes much longer and thus supplies of nitrogen and other salts are often deficient. Permafrost also inhibits aeration so necessary for plant growth.

All life is completely dependent on solar energy. Arctic eco-systems owe their existence to plants which trap solar radiation and convert it to plant production. "Although tundra plant pro-ductivity is low when compared with other world biomes," says botanist Dr. L. C. Bliss, "daily productivity during the short growing season (*ca.* 40 to 70 days) and the rates of efficiency of carbon fixation are comparable to many herbaceous com-munities of temperate regions."[1]

Tundra ecosystems are said to be "biologically fragile." There is a peak of plant and animal growth in the short summer followed by a long period of little or no biological production. On top of this seasonal cycle are superimposed other biological cycles, such as those of the lemming and the arctic hare, with a three to five year pattern.

Most truly arctic plants are perennial. The short summers sometimes do not allow time to complete the life cycle in a season. If one seed crop failed, it might be fatal for the species. Some species do not rely on seed production and are able to reproduce vegetatively–which is much more reliable under harsh conditions.

Growth is extremely rapid following the general snow melt. This is possible because of the large amounts of carbohydrates and starches stored in roots and rhizomes. Growth may occur at low temperatures, and during unfavourable periods of weather the growing parts of plants may actually freeze, but the plant is not killed.

Mosses, algae, lichens, and flowering plants are found as far north as there is land. For example, on Ellesmere Island, north of the eightieth parallel, herbs, grasses and willows are abundant enough to furnish food for herds of large mammals such as caribou and muskoxen. An estimated 500 species of flowering plants occur in the Canadian Arctic and about 800 species in the entire Arctic.

When the tundra bursts into bloom, purples, yellows, whites, reds, and pinks contrast with the greens and grays. Rhododendrons, heather, saxifrage, cotton grass, anemone, willow and arctic poppy are some of the most conspicuous plants.

Lichens are possibly the most important element of tundra vegetation, making up an average of thirty per cent of the plant cover and in some areas up to ninety per cent. The cladonia, popularly known as the reindeer lichen or caribou moss, is the mainstay of the caribou, one of the most important large mammals of the tundra.

Plants, the primary producers, provide the base for other forms of life. The total quantity of living material in the Arctic is low. This, coupled with low rates of annual production, favours an ecosystem with relatively few species. Such a system is thought to be unstable and easily disrupted.

Insects are found in great numbers in northern Canada. There are about 500 species of insects north of the tree-line. On the tundra, flies are most abundant, both in species and individual numbers, and they comprise a dominant part of insect life. They are a prime source of food for many arctic birds, especially shorebirds. There are just four species of mosquitoes in the Arctic, but their numbers are legion. The males feed on plant juices, the females on any warm-blooded animal. There are crane-flies, blackflies, hover-flies—even twenty species of butterflies and six species of fleas.

The Arctic is one of the most famous and important waterfowl "nurseries" in North America. Millions upon millions of ducks, geese and swans take up temporary residence to nest and raise their young. Along the coast of the Beaufort Sea more than a million king and common eiders may be seen during migration and when they are moulting. A large proportion of the breeding population of white geese is found in Canada's Arctic, including the entire population of Ross's goose.

The tundra world supplies three major elements for successful waterfowl production: space, habitat (lakes, rivers, and coast lines) and a readily available food supply.

Some species nest singly, while others congregate in large colonies. The colony nesters are especially vulnerable to interference by man. An aircraft flying low over the colony might cause serious disruption. Nesting habitat might be destroyed, even in winter, by tracked vehicles crushing the hummocks of vegetation found in nesting areas.

The brown, black and white Canada goose is found over most of the northern mainland, only occasionally on the Arctic Islands. It nests near water, favouring small islands often found in ponds and lakes. Four to six eggs are laid. There are ten subspecies of Canada geese, the largest being almost twice the size of the smallest.

The Dewey Soper Migratory Bird Sanctuary on the Great Plain of Koukdjuak, Baffin Island, is thought to be the largest goose nesting colony in North America. Approximately a half million blue geese nest there along with snow geese, lesser Canada geese (about 50,000) and black Brant. In late summer up to one and one-half million geese may use the area as a staging ground in preparation for the fall flight south. The west side of Bylot Island harbours a critical nesting area for about one-third of the world population of greater snow geese—20,000 out of 75,000 individuals. The snow and blue geese are colour phases of one species.

Walk out on the seemingly lifeless tundra in June and early July and in many places you'll be "surrounded" by circling, calling shorebirds. You may hear the nasal "he-haw he-haw" of the stilt sandpiper, the grating "toy toy toy" of the godwit, the melodious "kleee-e-e" of the golden plover or the loud, rolling "kur-leeu-u-u" of the whimbrel.

The most famous of the arctic shorebirds is the eskimo curlew. Once thought to be extinct, there have been several sightings in recent years in the southern United States and on the breeding grounds in the region of the Anderson River of the Northwest Territories. Author-naturalist Fred Bodsworth immortalized this rarest of North American birds in *The Last of the Curlews*. The Canadian Wildlife Service is undertaking field studies and surveys in an attempt to determine if there is still a vestigial breeding population.

About thirty species of shorebirds nest in Canada's Arctic. The most widely distributed are the semipalmated, golden and black-bellied plovers; ruddy turnstone; lesser yellowlegs, pectoral, white-rumped, Baird's, and least sandpipers; dunlin; sanderling; and northern phalarope.

Shorebirds often seem to be about the last birds to arrive and the first to leave. Of all the birds that nest in the Arctic they seem to have the shortest "turn-around" time. Some species build nests in grassy hummocks or on "islets" in the tundra ponds; others fashion a scrape in the ground and line it with small stones and bits of vegetation. It is believed that many adult shorebirds leave the nesting grounds soon after the eggs are hatched—in the case of the adult male perhaps even sooner. As the young shorebirds are born virtually ready to look after themselves, this departure of the adults may not be a sign of parental neglect but of an adaptation to lessen the competition for food in the immediate vicinity of the nest site.

Another rare northern nester is the famed whooping crane.

The entire world population nests in Wood Buffalo National Park on the border between Alberta and the Northwest Territories. Post-breeding whoopers may wander farther north during the summer.

The most abundant arctic sea-bird is the penguin-like thick-billed murre. Leslie Tuck of the Canadian Wildlife Service estimates there are about five million breeding murres in the eastern Canadian Arctic. One of the largest colonies, or loomeries, is at Cape Hay on Bylot Island, where about 400,000 pairs breed. Other loomeries are found on Baffin Island, Coats Island, Somerset Island and Cobourg Island. The murres play an important, but not fully understood, role in providing nutrient salts, such as potash, which stimulate growth of small marine organisms, to the extent that one authority has referred to their colonies as "the fertilizer factories of the northern seas."[3]

Two large birds of prey, the peregrine falcon and the gyrfalcon, are in danger of extinction. They are flesh eaters, and the cumulative effects of pesticide residues which have been found in the eggs, fat, and tissues of these falcons are thought to be the cause of the decline. The peregrine is extinct in eastern North America. The last stronghold for these magnificent birds is arctic Canada, Alaska, and the British Columbia coast. Both these species should be given full protection, as their survival is of international concern.

One of the best known arctic birds is the snowy owl, perhaps best known as "Ookpik." These large white owls make excursions south every four years or so, when their food supply, principally the lemming, suffers a population "crash." Fortunately, the snowy owl does not appear to be threatened by pesticides as are many other birds of prey, possibly because of its diet. Unlike most owls it is active during the daylight hours.

The symbol of the living Arctic is the majestic great ice-bear, or as it is usually called, the polar bear. Polar bears are found around the top of the world, on arctic islands and mainland coasts and on ice floes in polar seas. Their range has contracted and serious depletions have occurred in the past fifty years, mainly the result of over-hunting. They are listed as a "depleted species" by the IUCN Survival Service Commission. Estimates of world population vary from five to ten thousand, perhaps more, but it is difficult to obtain precise information. The polar bear stands at the pinnacle of the polar pyramid of predators, living mainly on seals. Only man can challenge the polar bear's supremacy, and then only with high-powered rifles.

Russia has given the polar bear total protection. Shamefully, Canada has recently allowed trophy hunting of polar bears. White hunters are taken out by Eskimos, who receive a fee paid to their village. The government excuse for allowing the hunting of polar bears is that it will bring much-needed revenue to the Eskimos. Yet the government refuses to recognize the Eskimos' aboriginal claims to the land.

The muskox, a shaggy survivor of the ice-age somewhat resembling the bison, is one of the most interesting and unique arctic mammals. It has a dark, heavy pelage which provides superb insulation against winter winds and temperatures. Musk-oxen are found on the mainland, but the bulk of the surviving population is on the Arctic Islands. On the mainland, the Thelon Game Sanctuary harbours the largest number, about 400. Ellesmere Island is thought to have a population of about 4,000, followed by Cornwallis, Melville and Axel Heiberg Islands with about 1,000 on each.

The muskox has been totally protected since 1917. It is believed that there has been a significant increase in population, which had been depleted by over-hunting. Present population estimates are 1,500 on the mainland and 8,500 on the Arctic Islands. There is growing concern that current exploration activities, especially the use of helicopters and small aircraft, may have adverse effects on muskoxen. Harassment by low flying aircraft may cause the muskoxen to stampede, causing death and disruption in the herd. Artificial barriers caused by thermal erosion may stop herds from reaching critical areas of their feeding range.

One of the most bizarre animals in the world is the single-tusked narwhal. These "unicorns of the sea" grow to at least 16 feet long and may weigh 6,000 pounds. The long spiral horn grows to a length of up to nine feet. The narwhal is the most arctic of all the whales, rarely leaving the arctic seas. It feeds on polar cod, halibut, northern shrimps and squid. Most of the estimated world population of about 10,000 is found in arctic Canada. Although they are not protected, they are not exploited commercially, except off the coast of Greenland.

Several species of seals are found in the polar seas, including the jar, bearded, harp, and hooded. Some seals migrate to avoid the perils of the frozen winter sea, but the jar and the bearded remain, utilizing breathing holes scratched out of newly formed ice. The seal is the main food supply for the polar bear. During the long winter, arctic foxes may scavenge seal carcasses left by the polar bears. Seals were also a major food item of the Eskimo.

"It is to be hoped that there will never be so few caribou that it will be possible to count them,"[4] wrote biologist C. H. D. Clarke in 1940. Unfortunately, the seemingly numberless herds of caribou dropped from several millions to about 250,000. The population seems to be on the increase, according to the Canadian Wildlife Service. Factors in its decline were greatly increased human exploitation, disease, and fires which destroyed a large part of its winter range. The caribou is a vital source of food and other necessities to the native people and with proper management could provide an important supply of meat for northern settlements.

There are several other species of mammals found in arctic Canada, including the arctic fox, prized for its fur; the walrus and grizzly bear, both in need of protection to ensure their survival; the lemming, famed for its dramatic population "explosions" and "crashes" and an important food source for snowy owls, jaegers, foxes and wolves; the right whale, of which only about 1,000 remain; and the beluga, or white whale.

The productivity of polar seas is much greater than that of the land, especially at the edge of ice in the zone where polar and warmer waters mix. Anadromous fishes, such as the arctic char and grayling, are important sources of food. It is estimated that there are about fifty species of fishes in the arctic seas. They are an important source of food for arctic mammals.

No reptiles are found in the Arctic and only one amphibian, the wood frog, is able to adapt to the Arctic and then only in the extreme southern limits.

The Arctic, by no means the lifeless desert it is thought to be, is characterized by a small number of species of both plants and animals. For example, of about 9,600 species of birds in the world, only eighty breed in the Arctic and few remain there year-round. There are around 3,200 species of mammals in the world; less than thirty are found on the tundra and in the polar seas. Of about 30,000 species of fish, only about fifty are thought to inhabit arctic seas. Arctic flora are also characterized by relatively few species when compared to more temperate regions.

Arctic ecosystems are often described as "youthful." Some scientists suspect that, at least in certain areas, these systems were much more diverse a comparatively short time ago. It is this lack of species diversity and the low annual productivity which makes the tundra so vulnerable to change, either natural or as a result of man's activities.

Dr. M. J. Dunbar suggests that lack of soils may be perhaps more important than low temperatures in accounting for the paucity of plant cover in the Arctic: "Smooth rock gives way to weathering and the working of lichens; pockets of coarse soil form, in which pioneer plants grow and increase the humus content; spiders and insects colonize the soil; these processes continue on substrates of different chemical natures until trees grow and larger animals invade the area. . . . As new species of

40

plants appear, the habitat complexity for animals increases, and new animal species open the way for new plants and animals, and the soil capital continues to grow. The most important ingredient is time."[5]

Time, however, is running out. Man and machines are moving into the north at an ever accelerating rate, threatening to destroy arctic ecosystems before man understands how they function and what part they play in the overall operation of the world's life-support system.

". . . the Arctic has problems for life which extend considerably beyond ice, snow and cold water."

M. J. Dunbar.

Ecological Development
in Polar Regions.

CHAPTER 3 / *The Importance of the Arctic to Science*

The 1970's are being hailed as the "age of ecology." In the Arctic man will see if ecology comes of age.

"Ecology is an integrating science concerned with the study of living things in their relationships with their environment," according to the United Natons Economic and Social Council. "Since man must co-exist with and is himself an integral part of a physical and biotic environment, ecology forms one kind of scientific basis for understanding man's role on earth."[1]

The earth's environment or biosphere–a thin film of water, air, and soil, on which all life depends–is made up of a number of ecosystems, each ecosystem consisting of plants, animals, microbes, and their abiotic, physical environs. These natural systems are dynamic, not static. The living matter, or biota, interacts with the environment and with other living organisms. These organisms have evolved intricate interdependencies in order to survive.

Ecological equipoise or balance is maintained by a complex web of consumers and consumables continually being cycled and re-cycled. Pollution does not exist as a characteristic of ecosystems. As ecologist Edward Deevey puts it: "For natural systems today's production was yesterday's garbage."

The Arctic may be of immense value to science as a vast outdoor laboratory, a sanctuary for survival. Arctic ecosystems are less complex than those of most other parts of the globe; they are still evolving, and they are for the most part undisturbed and unspoiled.

Canada's Arctic is not entirely an "unknown country" scientifically. A broad spectrum of studies have been carried out over a long period of time, mainly by various departments and agencies of the federal government. For example, the Geological Survey of Canada has surveyed most of the Arctic, both the mainland and the archipelago, and sponsored the Polar Inter-continental Shelf Program; the National Research Council has conducted exhaustive studies of permafrost and the problems it poses to development; the Canadian Wildlife Service has studied many arctic mammals, such as polar bear, muskoxen, arctic fox and caribou, and several species of birds; the Fisheries Research Board of Canada has investigated the salt and freshwater fishes and productivity of northern seas; the Defense Research Board maintains a station in the high Arctic at Hazen Lake; the National Museum has conducted floral and faunal surveys at many locations across the Arctic; and the Department of Transport operates a network of weather observatories.

Private organizations such as the Arctic Institute of North America, and a number of universities, operate research stations or have undertaken specific projects. For example, the Arctic Institute maintains a station at Cape Sparbo on Devon Island and has supported many projects, the University of Saskatchewan has an "Arctic Research and Training Centre" at Rankin Inlet, and the University of Western Ontario's station on the McConnell River is engaged in a long-term study of Canada geese and other waterfowl.

For the most part, however, research has been in the physical and earth sciences. The major thrusts have occurred in the areas which have a fairly direct relationship to economic development and resource exploitation. Unfortunately there has been little probing of the productivity of the living Arctic and few attempts to fathom the intricate interlocking and interdependent workings of the Arctic ecosystems.

In July of 1967, a world-wide co-operative study, the International Biological Program (IBP) began operation. The major objectives were studies of: (1) organic production on the land, in the freshwaters, and in the seas, so that adequate estimates might be made of the potential yield of new as well as existing natural resources, and (2) human adaptability to the changing conditions. Such a program of research was considered urgent because of the rapid rate of increase in the "numbers and needs of the human populations of the world" and because of the changes taking place in all environments throughout the world.

It was the hope of the IBP organizers that studies would be undertaken on all of the major ecosystems of the world. As Canada contains the world's largest area of arctic tundra, it was expected that Canada would sponsor a tundra study. But such was not the case. The federal government turned a deaf ear to proposals for such a study. Instead, it sponsored a study of grasslands in southern Saskatchewan–the Matador Project. It did become slightly involved in arctic studies with a freshwater productivity study on Cornwallis Island and a joint circumpolar human adaptability study of Eskimos at Igloolik. Unfortunately, three years of tundra ecosystem research, so vital to man's understanding and working in the Arctic, were lost.

In April 1969, Dr. Lawrence C. Bliss, a University of Alberta botanist, convened a meeting at Calgary to determine the feasibility of a Canadian tundra study. Following discussions throughout the summer and early fall, it was agreed during the International Conference on the Productivity and Conservation of Circumpolar Areas (held at Edmonton, Alberta in October 1969) to develop a High Arctic Tundra Productivity and Manipulation Study on Devon Island. This location was chosen for four reasons: the previous and current research in biology and glacial geology; the diversity of plants and animals in a relatively small valley with its own drainage basin, and uplands with sparse vegetation and animals; the herd of muskoxen, which would provide a large mammal as an important part of the study; and the fact that no other country could develop a High Arctic study and that Devon Island is representative of much of the High Arctic.

"If we are to know the limits of man's manipulation of tundra areas," asserts Dr. Bliss, "we must first know how these natural ecological systems function and how much variation there is from year to year in terms of plant and animal growth, fluctuations in population size, and the influence of environmental factors on animals and plants."[2]

This "base-line" research requires a new type of approach–termed "big-biology"–involving the use of teams of researchers from many disciplines working on all the components of an ecosystem and the interactions that occur between them. Among those participating in the High Arctic Tundra Study (HATS) will be ecologists, meteorologists, biologists, glaciologists, ornithologists, entomologists, soil scientists, paleoecologists, botanists, geologists, biochemists, physiologists, engineers, along with a number of graduate students.

The major areas of "base-line" research include: factors controlling the growth of plants; rates of plant photosynthesis and respiration; rates of mineral uptake and utilization by plants; rates of plant and animal decomposition and release of minerals; determining rates of heat, light and water vapour fluxes in an arctic ecosystem and how the various environmental factors influence plants and animals in terms of growth rates and population size; the role of soil insects and bacteria in decomposition of organic matter and the cycling of minerals; heat flux in relation to permafrost and depth of summer thaw;

46

rates of energy utilization by various birds and mammals; rates of soil formation in relation to topography and plant and animal communities; and determining the size of the various eco-system compartments and the rates of transfer between them.

Once these base-lines are established, says Dr. Bliss, "one can stress the system in terms of surface disturbances, manipulation of the size of animal populations and disturbances of animal populations in terms of noise, presence of humans, etc."[3]

Manipulatory research will include: rate of natural plant establishment following disturbance of the surface by such things as tracked vehicles, roads, fire, oil spills and use of hovercraft; rate of permafrost thaw following surface disturbance; developing methods and materials for "resealing" surface disturbances (testing native plant life and introducing new plant species, mulches, etc.); comparing the effect of surface disturbance on the basis of kinds of vehicles, time of year, soils, and plant cover; studying the rate of decomposition of oil following spillage into streams, bays, sea ice and various land surfaces; influence of oil on plants and animals when it is dumped into a bay or on land; ways of disposing of garbage, sewage and trash (such as lagoon, "hot-pot," plastic bags on sea ice, etc.); and the effect of noise, including land and ice-pack seismic lines, on bird and mammal populations.

The High Arctic Tundra Study was envisaged as a co-operative undertaking, staffed by various university, government and industry scientists and supported by the federal government, the oil industry, and private foundations. Base camp facilities are provided by the Arctic Institute of North America.

The federal government is now involved in northern ecological research through the Arctic Land-Use Research (ALUR) program, sponsored by the Department of Indian Affairs and Northern Development. In announcing the program in May 1970, DIAND Minister Chrétien said "we needed a comprehensive, mission oriented research program dealing with northern land-use problems to back up the Land-Use Regulations."

ALUR's specific objectives are "to detect and define environmental problems associated with land-use resulting from northern resource development; and to compile base-line information on undisturbed northern eco-systems."[5]

A number of Canadian Universities are participating in the ALUR program on a contract basis. The program has been provided with a budget of $500,000 per year for three years, beginning in 1970–71.

After preliminary field investigations during the summer of 1969, officials of the Northern Development Branch of DIAND decided that three land-use research sites would be needed. Land-Use Research Establishment (LURE) 1 is located in the boreal forest region of the Liard river basin; LURE 2 on Richards Island in the sensitive tundra zone of the Mackenzie river delta; and LURE 3 in the precambrian zone between Great Slave and Great Bear lakes.

Arctic ecosystems are regarded as relatively simple systems compared to those of more temperate zones. Why this is so is by no means clear. The most obvious answer, that cold was the basic cause, has come under critical examination recently and has been largely rejected. As M. J. Dunbar points out, in the sea and in lakes the temperature range is not extreme throughout the year and there is a growing body of evidence that metabolic adaption to low temperature is not as difficult to achieve as was originally believed. The situation on land is strikingly different. The severity of the long polar winter is such that plants and animals must take drastic measures to ensure their survival–in most cases they either remain dormant or migrate.

Growth rates in arctic plants and cold-blooded animals tends to be slow. Sometimes when there is an advantage in an accelerated growth rate, as in the larval stages of some aquatic insects, growth rates may be speeded up–in some instances to levels well above those of normal rates in more southern latitudes.

Scientists suggest that two basic factors probably are responsible for the simplicity of arctic ecosystems and that these are interrelated: namely, the small amount of annual growth of living matter and the "youthfulness" of the systems.

This so-called "youthfulness" of arctic ecosystems is dramatically illustrated by the general paucity of well developed soils. This is especially true in areas that were covered by ice-sheets during the last glacial periods. There is a considerable body of opinion that supports the view expressed at the end of the foregoing chapter, that lack of soil, and the slow rate of soil accumulation, may be of greater importance than the cold in explaining the rate of development of plant cover in the Arctic.[6] Experimental treatment of this question is vitally needed, both in the field and in the laboratory. The Arctic Controlled Environment Greenhouse at the University of Alberta would be well suited to the latter task.

The reversibility of the processes of ecological evolution are of great interest and there is no better place for their study than the Arctic. It is rather well known that the micro-ecosystems of certain areas of the Arctic were much more diverse a comparatively short time ago (geological time that is) than they are now. Because paleontological techniques have been developed for only the larger vertebrates there is a general lack of information on the disappearance or displacement of species. However, in the "ice-free refugia" and in the regions adjacent to the ice-sheets, animal species existed a few thousand years ago that are not now found in these regions. These species have not been replaced by some other species. The result, therefore, is probably a reduction in ecological diversity or, at the least, a drop in the total number of species.

As might be expected, the reasons for the disappearance of these animals are clouded by controversy. Of prime consideration is the phenomenon of climatic change, especially a sudden change which did not allow time for the species to adapt. What is needed is an accelerated program of paleontological research to probe back to the beginnings of the glacial periods and even beyond. This may supply at least some answers to the question of the ways in which the arctic ecosystems have developed and have been changed and modified by natural processes. Such studies would be of great importance to the development of general ecological theory.

Almost all of the research discussed to this point will require relatively sophisticated techniques and equipment. However, there is also a desperate need for some old-fashioned nature study, or observational natural history. In keeping with the times, we might best say that what is needed is an ecological survey of the Arctic–we simply must know the geographical distribution of plants and animals in arctic Canada.

A start has been made by the Canadian Wildlife Service with the publication in early 1971 of the *Arctic Ecology Map Series,* which consisted of twenty-six maps, covering much of Arctic Canada, with a booklet of detailed information keyed to each map. The prime purpose was to identify and map "important" and "critical" areas in arctic Canada where man's incursions might have destructive impact on wildlife populations or destroy wildlife habitats. The objectives were: (1) "to bring together as much data as possible on habitats utilized by a wide range of species," and (2) "to provide a planning tool for both government and industry to help preserve these wildlife areas."[7] The Canadian Wildlife Service sounds a note of caution in its introduction to the maps: "Since the Canadian Arctic is a vast, largely unknown area, the maps must be considered preliminary."[8] And the maps do not delineate the distribution of species –they show only the key areas of special importance.

There are two fundamental categories–"important" and "critical"–used in the *Arctic Ecology Map Series.* These coded categories, along with the descriptive report, explain why an area has been identified as important or critical, with all available information on the species of bird or mammal found there and, when possible, some indication of numbers. Both these categories "represent habitat necessary to the maintenance or survival of wildlife populations." For example, arctic Canada supports most of the known world population of such species as muskoxen, and harbours a large proportion of the North American breeding population of white geese. In this light, the potential impact of the destruction or serious disturbance of the habitat—and of possible breeding failure—should be cause for grave concern.

Canadians are all too familiar with the stories of how prodigal pioneers played an unwitting but nevertheless deadly role in wiping out such species as the passenger pigeon, the great auk and the Labrador duck; and in reducing the numbers of other species, such as the buffalo and the prairie chicken, almost to the point of no return. There is no excuse for this to be repeated in Canada's Arctic, but unless there is immediate government action—based on adequate scientific studies—some species, such as the muskox and the barren ground grizzly, may be seriously endangered. Other species, such as polar bear, barren-ground caribou, arctic fox, some marine mammals like the narwhal, walrus and beluga, might suffer from interference by man, especially during the critical breeding and "calving" periods.

Canada has a responsibility to the world community to safeguard all species found in her north. The World Biosphere Conference, held at Paris, France, in September 1968, suggested that all countries of the world make special efforts to preserve the rich genetic resources that have evolved over millions of years and are now being lost as a result of human actions, and once lost can never be recovered. The conference recommended that international efforts must include:

(1) "Preservation of representative and adequate samples of all significant ecosystems in order to preserve the habitats and ecosystems necessary for the survival of populations of the species;

(2) Establishment of special protected areas in regions where long-

domesticated species of plants and animals thrive in their original habitat;

(3) Strenuous efforts to protect the remnant populations of rare and endangered species of plants and animals, and to provide the care and conditions necessary for increase of their numbers, for their selection, and for their improvement."[9]

The Canadian Wildlife Service has taken that all-important first step towards an Arctic Ecological Survey. The federal government should immediately build on this base and authorize and fund an Arctic Ecological Survey that will be a model for the world.

For the past several hundred thousand years, the climate of the earth has fluctuated enough to produce a series of ice ages and warm interglacial periods. Until quite recently it was thought that these climatic changes were gradual; now, however, new theories have been put forth suggesting that they may occur with devastating suddenness.

The most dramatic of these sees a major part of the antarctic ice sheet slipping into the sea, thus raising the levels of the world's oceans from sixty to a hundred feet. It is suggested that this might occur in a week or two or it might take as long as forty years. In any event, if such a thing did occur, it would leave most of the world's cities under water.

Another theory now being widely discussed (quite recently by Prime Minister Trudeau), sees the melting or disturbance of the "thin" covering of ice on the Arctic Ocean as the signal for the start of a new ice age. This melting might occur if there were three or four unusually warm summers, when the sun is rich in sunspot activity and thus delivering more energy to earth than usual. It might possibly occur due to man-made, or at least man-initiated changes—such as a massive oil spill or the so-called "green-house effect" due to increased carbon dioxide in the atmosphere.

An ice-free Arctic Ocean would soon cause radical changes in the climate of the Northern Hemisphere and perhaps even the world. The land areas surrounding that ocean are now largely desert-like because there is so little precipitation, The on-shore winds have crossed a frozen sea and are not moisture-laden. But if the ocean were not frozen, these winds would pick up moisture and produce almost continuous snows on all high ground in their path, which would be the start of immense ice-sheets and ultimately initiate a new ice-age.

Removal of the arctic ice-pack would, according to two leading arctic scientists, Maurice Ewing and William L. Donn, cause four direct changes to occur:

[1] "A marked increase in the transfer of heat from ocean to atmosphere—most pronounced in winter.

[2] A mixing of water to the extent that the warm, saline Atlantic ocean water would not plunge several hundred yards below the colder, fresher Arctic ocean water as at present, but tend to mix with it.

[3] A replacement of the present, feeble, density driven Arctic circulation by a vigorous, wind driven circulation—probably in such a direction that the Atlantic-Arctic interchange of water would be greatly increased. This might well enable the Arctic ocean to remain ice-free, while supplying great quantities of heat and moisture to the polar atmosphere.

[4] A cooling of the Atlantic ocean and a warming of the Arctic ocean from an increased interchange of water."[10]

Since the arctic ice-pack is already afloat, sea levels would not be affected immediately—just as the melting of an ice cube in a glass of water does not raise the level. However, the resulting climatic changes are potentially disastrous. A number of world weather experts are of the opinion that this arctic ice-pack has a "judo-hold" on the world's climate. In addition to the examples cited previously it is believed that if the pack vanished the storm paths that carry rain to America's mid-west—the so-called "bread-basket of America"— would probably move north, possibly turning this region into a desert.

To bring about long-term changes, the Arctic Ocean would have to remain ice-free for a considerable period of years—

which is possible under certain circumstances. Some other possible consequences of an ice-free Arctic ocean are:

(1) An increase in precipitation, particularly in winter, on a broad circumpolar zone, with probable accumulation of ice-sheets in Eurasia and North America.

(2) A warming effect on lands immediately adjacent to the Arctic Ocean due to the influence of the relatively warm ice-free border zone.

(3) A major change in the pattern of arctic atmosphere circulation, because warming by open ocean would probably change the present polar high to a polar low–present clockwise circulation would be reversed to counterclockwise.

(4) A mid-latitude cooling resulting from growth of new ice-sheets. This would narrow the present climatic zones, thus producing greater temperature and moisture contrasts and would shift the present mid-latitude storm belt to the subtropic zone.

(5) A general global refrigeration resulting from the increased reflectivity of sunlight from the glaciated areas and the cloud-covered pluviated areas.

(6) A gradual lowering of the sea level as ice-sheets build up.

If the arctic ice-pack does indeed have a "judo-hold" on climate, what is the key to the delicate balance between melting and remaining frozen? Some scientists suggest a correlation between the long-term sunspot cycle and recent weather trends. However, the range of observations is not enough to rule out coincidence, and, also, the variations in solar energy production appear to be slight. Another theory links the ice-ages with changes in the tilt of the axis of the earth and the time of year when the earth is closest to the sun. Both influence the total amount of solar energy falling on high latitudes.

Yet another theory is that the amount of warm Gulf Stream water flowing into the Arctic Ocean over the shallows between Iceland and Norway is the limiting factor. When the Arctic Ocean is frozen and glaciers melt, the oceans receive water from the melting ice until enough warm water enters the Arctic

Ocean to reduce its ice cover to the vanishing point. This is said to "shift the climatic gears" and a new cycle is started. Snow storms "born" in the Arctic Ocean start a new ice-age, which takes water from the oceans until flow into the Arctic is curtailed. The Arctic Ocean then re-freezes and the glaciers again begin to melt.

Of critical concern is whether man-made pollution might tip the scales and initiate a melting of the arctic ice-pack. The influence of pollution, which has become a global problem, is relatively unknown–but efforts must be made to greatly expand man's knowledge of the potential threats pollutants pose. Already, earth satellites are able to measure incoming solar energy and outgoing energy losses over the globe, including the arctic ice-pack and open polar seas. Computer simulations may show what factors might lead to an ice-free Arctic Ocean and what effects this might have.

While it is clear that the Arctic is important to science, the issue of the importance of science to the Arctic is still clouded. Science has much to learn from the study of arctic ecosystems and its flora and fauna. In fact, the Arctic might best be seen as a vast outdoor laboratory where the basic secrets of the complex natural systems of the globe may at last be discovered and understood. On the other hand, a program of scientific research, undertaken before man causes widespread irreversible damage, might provide the basis for rational economic development of the Arctic. For the first time in the history of the world there could be necessary economic development without unnecessary environmental destruction.

Needless to say, such a program of research will take time, money, and skilled scientists. In a wealthy and highly developed country like Canada, there is no question that the money and the men are readily available. Whether or not there is time will depend on how serious Prime Minister Trudeau is in his pledge to preserve "the peculiar ecological balance of the Arctic" for mankind.

"There is no doubt that oil, its produc-tion, transportation, and the burning of its products creates more pollution than any other single factor."

H. K. Roessingh, Editor,

Canadian Petroleum

CHAPTER 4 / *Polar Pollution*

The recent technological and industrial invasion of the north poses potentially serious threats to arctic ecosystems. Flaring of "sour" natural gas or petroleum produces air pollutants that could have disastrous effects on the tundra's protective covering of plants. An oil spill could wipe out great numbers of birds and other animals. Tracked vehicles and bulldozers disturb vegetable cover, exposing the frozen ground and often causing "thermal erosion." And seismic "shots" may adversely affect populations of mammals and fishes.

Air Pollution

The "oxides" of carbon, nitrogen and sulphur are among the most dangerous and destructive pollutants found in the air. They are produced, in good part, when petroleum or its products are burned. Under some conditions they are hazardous to human health and they may seriously affect plants, trees and even some metals.

Lichens thrive in the extreme environmental conditions found in the Arctic because they are able to absorb from the atmosphere a wide variety of substances necessary for their survival. Although they are usually minor components of plant communities, they make up about thirty per cent of the vegetative cover of the tundra, and in some situations as much as ninety per cent. Lichens are the most important food source of the caribou.

"Apparently, the same physiological adaptations that enable lichens to thrive in barren, inhospitable habitats also make them vulnerable to destruction by air pollution," according to Drs. Edmund Schofield and Wayne L. Hamilton of Ohio State University's Institute of Polar Studies.[1]

Lichens are "dual-organisms" consisting of a fungus and an alga that live together in self-supporting, symbiotic association. The purpose of the fungus is to envelop, protect and supply the alga with moisture; while the alga multiplies by cellular division and manufactures food for the whole lichen by absorbing carbon dioxide from the air, and "building" it into starch through the action of water and solar energy.

Investigations in various parts of the world–France, England, United States, Sweden, and Canada–have shown that air pollution, especially sulphur dioxide, destroys lichens. Apparently the sulphur dioxide degrades the chlorophyll of the algal partners of the lichens, thus depriving them of the capacity to produce food. Lichens are conspicuously absent from most urban-industrial areas. The first to be affected, and thus the most sensitive, are usually the reindeer lichens, or cladonia–the ones found most commonly on the tundra.

Meteorological conditions may add to the dangers from air pollutants. Schofield and Hamilton describe them:

> In addition to the frequent occurrence of fogs on the Arctic Slope, particularly near the coast, further meteorological conditions must be taken into account. During much of the year, especially in winter, strong temperature inversions exist in the surface layers of the Arctic atmosphere. They are the result of strong negative radiation balance at or near the surface. When temperature in-

creases upward in the atmosphere, as it does in an inversion, the air mass is stable. Corrective overturning is impossible, the pollutants introduced into the inversion layer are dispersed only by diffusion and turbulence associated with horizontal wind. In regions of low topographic relief, wind turbulence is small, so that during times of inversions on the north Alaskan coastal plain conditions are optimal for the entrapment of smoke and fumes in a very thin blanket at the surface. Fogs or ice-fogs frequently develop during times of inversions. The associated water droplets or ice particles form on contamination particles and, in addition, scavenge pollutants from the air. Thus, contaminants become associated with larger particles and do not diffuse away as readily. When fog particles impinge on the surface, they stick either as dew or hoar frost. In this way, contaminants can be deposited on sensitive plants.[2]

Ice-fogs often occur in the Arctic, especially near the coast. Geophysicist C. Benson studied the ice-fogs near Fairbanks, Alaska, and concluded that "fall-out" from a polluted ice-fog would bring sulphur compounds from about half the fog-layer into direct contact with plants on the ground.

If a "Fairbanks-type" ice-fog formed near a well-site, when the wind was less than one mile per hour, the sulphur dioxide concentration could reach 0.05 parts per million or greater over an area of about forty square miles within four days if crude oil (or natural gas) were burned at the rate of about a thousand pounds per hour. This is roughly equivalent to burning 110 gallons of gasoline per hour—which is reasonably close to the fuel consumption to be expected of a drill site with heated buildings, tractors, power generators, and heaters for warming drilling-mud and crude oil.

Over two hundred wells will be drilled in Canada's north during 1971-72, as compared to sixty in 1969. Following Imperial Oil's Atkinson Point find and Panarctic's gas discoveries, interest has greatly increased. Several large international oil companies, such as BP Oil, Elf Exploration, Sun Oil and

Deminex, have active drill rigs on the islands or the Mackenzie Delta. In the opinion of R. A. Hemstock, Imperial's Arctic Coordinator, the development of all the potential Arctic oil lands would involve the drilling of 700 to 1,400 wildcat wells and 6,000 to 12,000 development wells. This would mean that large amounts of hydrocarbon fuel will be burned down north. And to this must be added the possibility of uncontrolled burning of crude oil or natural gas if a wildcat well blows out of control, as Panarctic's L-67 did twice.

Another factor is the greatly increased air traffic–both for freight and passengers–including jets (737's) and turbo-props. Engine exhausts from jets, on arrival and departure, average about 140 pounds of sulphur oxides, nitrogen oxides, hydrocarbons, particulate matter, and carbon monoxide.

The air pollutants produced by this unprecedented activity may have already had serious effects on tundra vegetation, at least in certain areas. Research is needed to determine what damage has been done, if any, and what levels of the various air pollutants are permissible. Consideration should be given to using low-sulphur oil or converting to natural gas. A monitoring and measuring network should be an integral part of arctic air pollution control. Ambient standards must be set and enforced–even to the extent of closing down exploration and production operations when high levels threaten the environment.

The miasmal mists of DDT have reached the Arctic borne by the winds. Polar bears have DDT in their flesh and the peregrine falcon and gyrfalcon may be threatened with extinction as DDT and other chemicals inhibit breeding. Radionuclides–Cesium-137 and Strontium-90–have been found in caribou and Eskimos.

Arsenic, released into the air from mining operations, is a problem at Yellowknife. Dr. R. E. Beschel of Queen's University believes it is chiefly responsible for the failure of lichens to regenerate on the rocks and trees within a radius of twelve or fifteen miles from that city.

Oil Spills

The possibility of an oil gush or spill exists from the time a wildcat well is spudded until the crude oil is finally delivered to the refinery.

At Cook Inlet, Alaska, an extraordinary series of oil pollution incidents followed the initial oil discovery in 1962. These now average two to four each months, ranging in severity from slight to extremely destructive. Tens of thousands of seabirds and waterfowl have been killed and commercial species of fish and bottom-dwelling crabs have been affected. There is growing concern for some of the mammals of the region—seals, sea otters, beluga whales and bears. A massive oil slick killed tens of thousands of ducks and seabirds off Point Barrow, Alaska.

Moving arctic oil to market will involve transporting it thousands of miles, by pipelines over hazardous terrain (underlain by permafrost), by tanker through the ice of frozen seas, or by submarine under the ice. If production is to be economic, oil companies must think in terms of 10,000-barrel-a-day wells, 2,000,000 barrel-a-day pipelines, 300,000-ton supertankers, and 175,000-ton submarines. Thus, if an accident occurs a large volume of oil is likely to be released.

Dr. A. H. Macpherson of the Canadian Wildlife Service, an internationally recognized authority on arctic wildlife, speculates that if a major oil spill occurred in the Arctic

> direct mortality of wildlife from a large oil gush or a tanker accident could be enormous. In spring heavy oil pollution in open water off the floe-edge in the Beaufort Sea or Hudson Bay would unquestionably trap very large proportions of the Arctic populations of swans, ducks, geese, gulls, guillemots, murres, fulmars, jaegers and phalaropes. Crude oil is toxic to many birds and would presumably be also to mammals attempting to remove it from their pelts with their tongues. Polar bears and Arctic foxes might suffer on the sea-coasts; muskrats, beavers, mink, otter and lesser species would doubtless be affected by a major spill on the Yukon River or in the Delta of the Mackenzie. Seals also appear vulnerable to crude oil spills. . . .[3]

Thick, dark crude oil spilled on the surface of the frozen Arctic Ocean would absorb sunlight, melting vast quantities of ice and possibly resulting in a flow of oil and water to the coasts and beaches of the northern islands and mainland. Experiments have been undertaken in which lampblack was spread over the ice to absorb solar heat; it has been suggested that this method might be used to melt glaciers on Greenland.

Oil and cold water certainly don't mix. And very little is known about the behaviour and effects of crude oil in this situation—but what little we do know is not reassuring. In a report "Environmental Effects of Oil Pollution in Canada," Dr. Richard Warner states:

> . . . decomposition (of oil) in the Arctic oceans, whose temperatures are at 0°C (32°F) or below throughout the year, would be very slow indeed. Where oil is exposed to still lower temperatures, for instance when carried onto shorelines and ice floes, biochemical decay would be virtually nonexistent, and the oil would persist for decades, perhaps centuries . . . . evaporation rates of the highly toxic 'lighter fractions' of crude oil slicks are believed to be greatly slowed. The net effect is to significantly prolong the time during which the sensitive marine organisms are exposed to the toxic influences of the lighter hydrocarbons. Mirinov has recently shown that such surface films or oil are especially toxic to the hyponeuston, that special marine community found in the surface layer of water (from 0 to 2 inches depth) and which is composed in part of the embryonic and larval stages of many pelagic and bottom dwelling forms. Many of the species inhabiting the hyponeuston during their early stages are of great value to commercial fisheries. . . . Planktonic algae (important producers of oxygen) have also been found sensitive to the toxic components of such oils, exhibiting retarded cell growth and direct mortality.[4]

The question of arctic oil spills should be considered in terms of "when an accident occurs," rather than "if an accident occurs." A great deal of research is required to determine the effects of such spills on the arctic environment. Dr. Warner recommends the following approaches to oil pollution problems—present and potential—in Canada:

1. Instigation of a biologically and oceanographically oriented research program in the North Atlantic and coastal regions of eastern Canada with special reference to seabirds and other important marine species.
2. Instigation of a research program into the biological effects of marine oil pollution upon the hyponeuston, or the surface and immediate subsurface biotic community which is so critical to the continued productivity of the oceans.
3. Instigation of a research program into the biological effects of oils in arctic and sub-arctic waters.
4. Carrying out a national survey to identify sites of special (ecological and scientific) importance, leading to development of critical area protection programs.
5. Instigation of a research program into the biological effects of present and proposed refinery and petrochemical plant operations (e.g. at Holyrood and Come-by-Chance).
6. Development of a truly effective national system for locating, reporting and identifying the sources of oil pollution circumstances.
7. Development of a National Contingency Policy.
8. Development of national criteria for environmental protection to be included in all oil leases, construction contracts and other agreements where the activity presents some probability of risk to the environment.
9. Improvement of international coordination and communications.

The Phenomenon of Permafrost

"Permafrost can never be considered alone," Dr. W. Pruitt told the World Tundra Conference, "either in its genesis and degradation or in its ecological effects. Permafrost forms a complex, dynamic system with climatic history, vegetation history, recent climate, present vegetation, substream, topography, solifluction and animal activity all interacting." Pruitt warned that "in permafrost regions, any human activity, especially one to be accompanied by modification of natural vegetation associations, should therefore be preceded by investigations to determine the changes to be anticipated in the permafrost regime."[5]

The serious problems posed by permafrost must be solved if technological man is to successfully exploit arctic oil and gas reserves. For example, let's examine the proposal to build a 1,700 mile long, four foot diameter pipeline from Prudhoe Bay, Alaska, to Edmonton, Alberta. The suggested route is across the top of the Yukon Territory, through the Mackenzie Delta to the vicinity of Inuvik and south along the Mackenzie River. The pipeline would pass through varied terrain—including mountains, polygonal networks formed by the melting of ice wedges, pingos (small ice-filled conical hills), thaw lakes and pits, and "beaded" drainage patterns.

Any disturbance of the tundra's vegetative cover and surface soil that insulates the permafrost from the sun, whether due to the passage of heavy tracked vehicles (some of the pipe-laying and transporting equipment weighs well over 100 tons or more when loaded) or to excavation and associated construction disturbance, may upset the delicate thermal regime and may cause severe thawing. This is especially true in areas where high-ice-content (supersaturated) permafrost occurs. The soil loses its ability to support a load and sinks as the water content melts away. Erosion carries off exposed matter. This "thermal erosion" can and sometimes does happen quite rapidly—within days, or even hours. This means that the supporting surface beneath the pipe could be washed out.

Dr. Arthur H. Lachenbruch of the U.S. Geological Survey notes that when full production is achieved the oil temperatures would be in the neighbourhood of 158 to 176 degrees Fahrenheit, and that such an installation could thaw the surrounding permafrost. "Where the ice content of permafrost is not high, and other conditions are favourable, thawing by the buried pipe might cause no special problems. Under adverse conditions, however, this thawing could have significant effects on the environment and possibly upon the security of the pipeline."

Lachenbruch estimates that a pipeline four feet in diameter buried six feet deep in permafrost and heated to 176 degrees F. would thaw a cylindrical region around the pipeline 20 to 30 feet in diameter in a few years in typical permafrost soil. And he believes that the principal effect of insulating the pipe would be "to increase oil temperature rather than to decrease thawing." Conservationists are concerned, he says, that "the prospect of a buried pipeline conjures pictures of an impassable 'canal' of unstable land, and of slides which could bring about ruptured sections of pipe and produce ruinous oil spills . . ."[6]

If a break occurred in the proposed four foot diameter pipeline, hot oil would gush out at the rate of about 500,000 gallons per mile of pipe. Although pipelines are equipped with "shut-off" valves, they are seldom placed closer than one mile. The hot oil, depending on the season and the local terrain and drainage patterns, might cause inestimable damage and would be almost impossible to clean up. Much of the lichen tundra would probably soak the oil up like a sponge; coupled with slow bacterial breakdown and evaporation it might take decades or centuries for the land to recover.

Engineers in the north have an axiom about permafrost—"Keep it frozen!" The simplest way is to lay an insulating pad over the surface of the ground or, in the case of buildings, put them on stilts. Gravel is commonly used as an insulating material and the pads may be several feet thick. To lay an insulating pad of gravel (ten feet wide and five feet thick) over 1,700 miles would require approximately 18,000,000 cubic yards of gravel. Over most of the route an access and service road must be built, with at least a hundred-foot right-of-way, to handle the "giant" equipment needed to haul and lay large diameter pipe. Also, gravel would be used in building airstrips for support aircraft, pumping stations and supply depots. This would increase the demand for gravel at least tenfold. In fact, gravel may become a key northern resource.

The Mackenzie Valley Pipeline Research Group is conducting an extensive program of research into the problems of building and operating "hot" oil pipelines in the north. At a site near Inuvik, 1,400 feet of large diameter pipe is being used for test purposes. It is estimated that it will take at least three years to complete the research.

Guidelines governing the future ownership, operation and ecological safeguards for northern oil and gas pipelines were announced in mid-August 1970 by Energy Minister Greene and Northern Development Minister Chrétien. Two of the seven guidelines are of importance for the conservation of the northern environment:

[1.] "Initially, only one trunk oil pipeline and one trunk gas pipeline will be permitted to be constructed in the North within a 'corridor' to be located and reserved following consultation with industry and other interested groups."

[2.] "The National Energy Board will ensure that an applicant for a certificate of public convenience and necessity must document the research conducted and submit a comprehensive report assessing the expected effects of the project upon the environment. Any certificate issued will be strictly conditioned in respect of preservation of the ecology and environment, prevention of pollution, prevention of thermal and other erosion, freedom of navigation and the protection of the rights of Northern residents, according to standards issued by the Governor in Council on the advice of the Department of Indian Affairs and Northern Development."[7]

Keeping in mind the fact that these are only guidelines, and the government's lack of success with guidelines in other fields, there are a number of pertinent questions which should be publicly answered before approval is granted for the construction of a northern pipeline:

1. How much time is needed to develop adequate information upon which to base the decision as to whether it should be built?

2. How much money should be spent on research on all aspects of the proposed pipeline? Who should finance it?
3. How much of the as yet unspoiled Yukon and Northwest Territories will be scenically defaced as a direct and indirect result of the pipeline project?
4. Is this pipeline in the public interest, as contrasted with the interest of the oil/gas industry? Would it be sounder public policy to exploit arctic oil/gas resources more slowly?
5. Exactly where is the pipeline going?
6. What will a 1,700 mile long "hot pipe" do to the permafrost regime? What will be the impact on the ecology of the surrounding lands?
7. What will gravel extraction, construction operations, communications and waste disposal do to the terrain, the rivers and streams and the wildlife?
8. How will this effect the great economic potential that outdoor recreation opportunities may provide?
9. What is the position of the land rights of Eskimos, Indians and Metis?
10. How much erosion might be caused by the project? How great, if any, is the risk of pipeline breakage by land slippage?
11. Are the new Northern Land Use Regulations, the guidelines announced by Greene-Chrétien, and other existing legislation and regulations, adequate to ensure protection for the northern environment?
12. What economic and social impact might the proposed pipeline "corridor" have beyond its original purposes? Will it function as a major transportation route?
13. How many people, with what education, experience and expertise, should be employed to evaluate, supervise and monitor such a project?

Some of the environmental problems encountered by the oil industry operating in the Arctic and sub-Arctic have been described by T. G. Watmore of Imperial Oil Limited. In October 1965, a bulldozer blade, which scraped no more than a foot of peaty surface soil and vegetation for seismic line on the Tuktoyaktuk Peninsula, originated some disturbing damage. Watmore reported in *Canadian Petroleum* that "thaw and settlement has produced a lengthy depression in the cutline which is more than six feet deep in places."[8] The eventual effect is that of a moat or trench. On sloping land this may create a new drainage channel and completely alter the existing ecological regime of the terrain it traverses.

One effect of these changes is the creation of barriers which may interfere with the movements of caribou herds–an important tundra mammal. Bulldozed lines on the Peel Plateau near Ford MacPherson were revisited and it was found that in four years a gully twenty-three feet wide and eight feet deep had developed on a three per cent slope over one and a half miles.

Scientists reported to the World Tundra Conference that surface damage in the Arctic, caused by seismic activity and cutting of roads and lines, was already widespread. J. K. Naysmith of the Department of Indian Affairs and Northern Development said that "last winter [1968-69] over 8,000 miles of seismic lines were cut and this may well increase to over 15,000 miles this coming winter [1969-70]."[9] On the Arctic Islands, Panarctic has shot at least 1,400 miles of seismic lines.

These seismic lines may disturb the surface vegetation and destroy its "insulating" qualities–exposing the permafrost to the air and sun. This may result in "thermal erosion," which sometimes severely alters the terrain. It may cause changes in drainage patterns, induce soil erosion and form barriers to migrating mammals. The end result may, in some cases, be irreversible changes in the ecological balance and permafrost regime–which took thousands of years to develop.

Charlie Gruben, an Eskimo delegate to the World Tundra Conference, gave the following eyewitness account of what was happening around his "home" near Tuktoyaktuk:

In our area . . . it is practically impossible now to live off trapping only. That is the impact of all ways of transport in our area, plane, helicopter, cat-trains on the tundra, seismic blasting on land and sea. Is this not a sufficient factor to disturb animal life in land and sea? Trails are visible from aircraft, all around our trapping ground. One year we had to send a protest as creeks were dammed and no fish were caught in the harbour of Tuktoyaktuk. This summer [1969] no whale were caught in our waters. Is this due to blasting (seismic operation)? We believe this operation has something to do with it. It is the first time in the history of Tuktoyaktuk that we do not harvest whales. . . .[10]

Water Pollution

In southern Canada and the United States, water pollution is a major environmental problem. Rehabilitating lakes and rivers will cost many billions of dollars. Most of this is caused by human and industrial waste.

The same pattern has emerged in the north. Raw sewage is dumped in the Yukon River at Whitehorse and into Hudson Bay at Churchill; mine effluent discharged into Baker Creek near Yellowknife has wiped out the local fishery for Grayling. Ecologist Ian McTaggart Cowan reports that the beaches of some of our most remote Arctic Islands are "littered with plastic bags of human excrement grounded ashore after drifting miles from some northern outpost of our culture."[11]

However, the Northern Inland Waters Act (Bill C-187) passed by the House of Commons on May 5, 1970, should prevent many of the problems of water pollution that plague southern society. According to Northern Development Minister Chrétien, the bill has four main purposes:

[1.] "To provide for the equitable distribution of sharing of rights to use water in the North among interests with legitimate and sometimes conflicting claims on this resource;
[2.] To ensure that the disposition or allocation of water rights is done in a manner that is consistent with immediate and long-term regional and national interest;

[3.] To ensure that all works and undertakings planned for the use, diversion, storage or treatment of water are designed and constructed to acceptable engineering standards; and

[4.] To establish and maintain the principle that rights to the use of water are dependent on the users accepting the full responsibility for maintaining its quality or restoring its quality to acceptable standards before returning the water to its natural environment."[12]

If the Northern Inland Waters Act is implemented and adequately enforced we would avoid the "after-the-fact" pollution situation which prevails over most of Canada. It is an extremely progressive piece of legislation, and the government and Mr. Chrétien deserve the highest praise for introducing it.

It should be realized, says Dr. W. A. Fuller, that "the cold, oligotrophic waters of most of the north do not have the ability to break down wastes as fast as richer, warmer waters in the south. Thus the carrying capacity for domestic waste of northern streams is less than that of a stream of equivalent size in a southern region."[13] Permafrost also complicates the waste disposal problem. It is difficult to dig disposal pits, and incineration of garbage could result in serious thawing of the underlying permafrost. Needless to say, sewage lagoons and mine tailings ponds are not too efficient at fifty degrees below zero; other disposal techniques and equipment may also prove inadequate under these severe environmental conditions.

Research is needed into the problems of treating human and industrial wastes under northern conditions. Dr. Fuller suggests that waste disposal might be one of "the major restraints on the development of a large metropolitan area in the northern parts. . . ."[14]

Mining

Prospecting for minerals and the development of mines have had a widespread impact on the northern environment. Mining is, at the moment, the major economic activity in the north.

Such activities as staking, line cutting, road building, drilling, and open-pit mining leave their mark on the land. Most of these activities are not subject to land use regulations.

While oil exploration has been subjected to the most criticism for scarring the landscape, mining exploration may have similar effects. Ecologist Douglas H. Pimlott describes the landscape surrounding Pine Point, on the south shore of Great Slave Lake, as being " 'neatly' divided into 1,500 foot squares for a distance of approximately 100 miles from the functioning mine."[16]

"The sites of hundreds of prospecting camps," says Dr. McTaggart Cowan, "are marked by tons of almost indestructible litter defiling even the most remote areas of the north."[17] And M.P. R. J. Orange, who represents the Northwest Territories, told the House of Commons that ". . . on Great Bear Lake, north of the Arctic Circle one can walk along the shore of the lake, which is 12,000 square miles and find places where people have left empty beer bottles, empty pork and bean cans, spam tins and other pieces of garbage."[18]

Mine sites, such as the one at Pine Point, present problems of large, ugly scars being left on the landscape if a rehabilitation program is not mandatory.

Biocides

Establishment of new communities in the north, either temporary or permanent, often leads to demands for control of mosquitoes, black flies and tabanids. Now that the use of DDT has been severely restricted other biocides will be substituted. Any chemical used should be thoroughly tested to determine its effects on the environment. Present licensing does not require any proof from the manufacturer that his product will not cause ecological harm. This must be changed, and the north is a good place to start. A permit system should be introduced to strictly control spraying.

To sum up, the northern environment may in the next few years face many of the threats that have caused so much environmental pollution and damage in the south. In addition, the fragile tundra is extremely susceptible to damage by physical disturbance and air pollutants. Pollution is a much more serious problem than in the south because of the slow rate of growth and the much slower rates of bacterial action. If the north is to be developed rationally, strict anti-pollution policies must be enforced. There is no excuse for "after-the-fact" solutions.

". . . somehow the gold isn't all."

Robert Service,

The Spell of the Yukon

CHAPTER 5 / *Tomorrow's Wilderness*

There are few places left on this gloomy globe where one may travel very far without finding some trace of technological man's interference with nature. Canada's north is one such place–a vast reserve of wilderness, a sanctuary for survival and, perhaps, sanity.

But this very vastness may be a major obstacle to setting aside large national parks and ecological research reserves. "What is more ludicrous in a country of this size and emptiness than people becoming passionate about preserving our wilderness?" asked puzzled sports-columnist Scott Young. What, indeed? However, Mr. Young would be hard pressed to show us even a vestige of the virgin pines that once covered much of eastern Canada, or a tract of long- or short-grass primitive prairie. They are gone for ever.

Wilderness might best be defined as "a remote area of un-settled land which is not yet being used for commercial pur-poses," according to ecologist Douglas H. Pimlott.[1] The United States Wilderness Act of 1964 considers wilderness "an area of undeveloped Federal land retaining its primeval character and influence, without permanent improvements or human

74

habitation, which is protected and managed so as to preserve its natural conditions."

Wilderness is more than just rocks, plants, animals, and water—more than just scenery. Wilderness is the opportunity to become attuned to the realities of nature, far removed from the artificialities of modern life. Wilderness is the opportunity to pit one's self against primitive conditions. And increasingly, wilderness is a place for plants and animals which have nowhere else to go.

Canada does not have a wilderness act or an official definition of wilderness. The lands that have been preserved on the national scene were set aside under the National Parks Act. The Act states that the parks are "dedicated to the people of Canada for their benefit, education and enjoyment" and that national parks "shall be maintained and made use of so as to leave them unimpaired for the enjoyment of future generations."[2] The Act is basically a good one and has been carefully administered over the years. All resource utilization is prohibited in national parks. Some of the best known national parks are Banff, Jasper and Wood Buffalo in Alberta, Point Pelee in Ontario, and Fundy in New Brunswick.

In early 1967 Arthur Laing, then Minister of Indian Affairs and Northern Development, told the annual meeting of the Canadian Audubon Society that there was no complete national park in the nearly forty per cent of Canada located in the Northwest Territories and the Yukon. Five years later there is still no complete national park north of the sixtieth parallel, the nearest approximation being Wood Buffalo National Park, which straddles the Alberta–Northwest Territories border.

In 1962, officials of the National Parks Branch carried out a field survey of national park potentials in the Northwest Territories and the Yukon. In a report apparently "for internal use only" and dated January 31, 1963, staff planners Lloyd Brooks and Harold Eidsvik recommended that three major national park reserves be set aside: the east arm of Great Slave Lake and Artillery Lake, the South Nahanni region, and the Donjek-Dezabeash (Kluane) region. The report stressed the importance of immediate action "to protect these prime park lands now while they are relatively virgin in character."[3]

No action was taken on setting aside any of the proposed areas, or even withdrawing them from disposal under the Territorial Lands Act and the Canada Mining Regulations.

The National and Provincial Parks Association of Canada passed a resolution at its second annual meeting (May 27, 1966) urging the government to act immediately to establish Great Slave Lake National Park. The Parks Association was of the opinion that the area was "only of marginal mining value"[4] but tremendously important for many species of wildlife, including caribou, barren-ground grizzly and muskox, and that the scenery was spectacular. The area around Artillery Lake and the eastern end of Great Slave Lake was the scene of a major mineral staking rush in 1968. Over 8,000 claims were staked but, as with so many "staking rushes," interest soon cooled and the speculators moved elsewhere. Finally, in January 1969, the government's National Parks Branch issued a formal proposal for Great Slave Lake National Park.

"There are strange things done 'neath the midnight sun," wrote Robert Service, and one of the strangest in recent times was this proposal for this Great Slave National Park.

Proposed was a "park in two parts," with a ten-mile-wide corridor between the parts. The park would be established on the basis of a "core" plus "reserve" concept. Two core areas with a total area of 1,100 square miles (600 and 500 square miles) would immediately be brought under the protection of the National Parks Act. In addition, a reserve area of 3,200 square miles (including the ten-mile corridor) in which the mineral potential is not fully known *might* be added to the core areas after a ten-year period during which exploration for minerals would be allowed. During this ten-year period the area

76

might be subjected to line-cutting, road building, drilling, and the other activities of mineral exploration. No matter how carefully supervised, this would likely result in some damage to the environment.

A public meeting was held on June 24, 1969, at St. Patrick's School in Yellowknife to discuss the national park proposed for the east arm of Great Slave Lake. Every major conservation association in Canada went on record, by brief, letter, or verbal presentation, as supporting the park proposal (with, of course, some provisos). Many of the conservation associations evidently received very short notice of the meeting–for example, the Canadian Audubon Society got its notice on June 16, just eight days before the meeting. And there were no details of the proposed park enclosed with the notice of the meeting.

While strongly supporting the concept of a national park in the area, the Canadian Society of Fisheries and Wildlife Biologists suggested that the present proposal was deficient in at least three ways:

1) Christie Bay, which includes the deepest freshwater in North America was not included–although it adjoins the western core area.
2) The most scenic part of the outstanding geological feature of the region, the MacDonald Fault, was not included in either the core or reserve areas and some of it should be preserved.
3) Only half of Artillery Lake was included in the core. Since the forest-tundra transition is perhaps the major ecological reason for preserving the area, and since this transition zone runs through the middle of the lake, all of Artillery Lake should immediately be included in the core.

The only major dissenting voice at the meeting was the Northwest Territories Chamber of Mines. In a terse, two page statement the Chamber claimed that "establishment of a National Park in the East Arm of Great Slave Lake will be detrimental to the economy of the N.W.T."[5] As might be expected, the Chamber of Mines believes that the area proposed for a park is one of great potential importance for mineral deposits. Many conservationists are of the opinion that no matter where a national park is proposed, mining interests will claim it is a prime area for minerals. The Chamber also mentioned the power potential of the Lockhart River, the importance of access to water routes for moving supplies and ore, and the number of jobs which might be created by mine development.

While the mining industry is not against national parks, it certainly was "against the location of this *particular* park."[6] (emphasis by N.W.T. Chamber of Mines). However, the Chamber suggested that a national park of 1,500 square miles might be established (the 3,200 reserve area would be eliminated) if the Government allowed "unrestricted rights to development of hydro power for all time" and "unrestricted access for all time through the park."[7]

The mining industry has long been opposed, privately but seldom publicly, to the establishment of large national parks, especially in the more northern parts of Canada. It is possible that the original bizarre proposal for a "park in two parts" was, at least in part, the result of pressure from the extremely powerful and wealthy mining interests. One important feature of public meetings and hearings on proposed parks is to flush the opposition out into the open for all Canadians to see and hear. Quite a contrast to some of the mining companies' and associations' slick commercials on radio and TV.

Finally, on March 24, 1970, under the authority of Orders in Council PC 1970-526 and 1970-527, lands containing 2,860 square miles were withdrawn from disposal under the Territorial Lands Act and the Canada Mining Regulations. However, this action does not prejudice the rights of the holders of mineral claims in good standing acquired prior to the above date.

What happens next depends to a large extent on how serious the federal government is in establishing Great Slave National

Park. But, no matter what, it will be a prolonged process to extinguish the thousands of mineral claims on land to which, only a few years ago, the Crown held all rights.

The same sad spectacle is happening with respect to the two other areas recommended in the 1963 Brooks-Eidsvik report. In April 1971, an area of 870 square miles was withdrawn under the Territorial Lands Act along the South Nahanni River, pending completion of a study to determine if the area is suitable as a future national park.

The National and Provincial Parks Association of Canada has urged that the Government of Canada establish a 10,120-square-mile national park in the south-western part of the Yukon, which means giving national park status to the existing Kluane Game Sanctuary. The National Parks Branch may soon propose a 700-square-mile national park in this area of the St. Elias Mountains, the highest range in North America, including Mount Logan, Canada's highest at 19,850. The *New York Times* quotes John I. Nichol, director of the National Parks Branch as saying that "You don't have to preserve the whole flipping range to attain the ends you want."[8] But no one has asked that the "whole flipping range" be preserved (although that might not be such a bad idea); conservationists simply feel that it is vital to secure an area large enough to protect one of North America's most varied wildlife populations—including wolves, grizzly bears, eagles, big horn sheep, wolverines, moose and caribou. Visitors to the 10,120 acre park proposed by the National Parks Association will be able to see many of these animals on alpine slopes close to the valleys, according to ecologist John Theberge.

The mining industry, predictably, has opposed the establishment of the Kluane park, despite the fact that mineral exploration in the area has been relatively light and nothing of promise has been found. A member of the executive of the Yukon Chamber of Mines, Ray McKamey, thinks that "with the new regulations on pollution control mining could be an asset to any park."[9] The lunar landscape at Sudbury, the strip mining at Canmore and the open-pit at Pine Point suggest otherwise.

It is worth noting that the original proposal for the three park reserves, made in January 1963, recommended that a total area of about 20,000 square miles should be set aside. The parks the National Parks Branch proposes are only 4,430 square miles–about one-quarter of the original total. If the three national park reserves had been established according to the original plan they would have covered the complete range of the major geological and ecological zones for half a million square miles across the southern sections of the Northwest Territories and the Yukon.

There are many other areas that should be included in a system of parks and reserves. The rich tundra in the Bathurst Inlet region, the desert-like landscape of much of Southampton Island, the coastal corridor of tundra plain and pingo area near Tuktoyaktuk, the glaciers and fiords of north-east Baffin Island, and major wildlife reserves such as Victoria Island for arctic char spawning streams and the Thelon Game Sanctuary for caribou and muskox are possible national parks suggested by John A. Carruthers, of the National Parks Branch. Some of the most spectacular and dramatic scenery in the world is found in the Yukon–the Mackenzie, the British and the St. Elias Mountains–and large mountain parks should be established there for the future.

In addition to an adequate system of national parks there must be a number of ecological research reserves set aside to provide scientists with living laboratories to study arctic ecosystems. A committee of the International Biological Program, chaired by Dr. W. Fuller, has recommended over fifty sites across the Arctic to the federal government. Although some investigations were being planned at one point, the government has not dedicated any of these areas as yet. The importance of a chain of research reserves of sufficient size to maintain the natural conditions free from interference is of prime importance if we are to develop an understanding of arctic ecosystems.

Canada has played a leading role in the efforts of the United Nations to grapple on a global scale with the effects of man's actions in changing the face of the earth. The U.N. General Assembly authorized a two-week World Conference on the Human Environment, to be held in June 1972, in Sweden. A noted Canadian, Dr. Maurice Strong, has been appointed Under-Secretary General of the United Nations, with special responsibility for environmental problems and chairmanship of the Conference on the Environment.

The purpose of the conference is to give practical encouragement, and provide guidelines for action by governments and those international organizations which have been designed to protect and improve the environment, and, through international co-operation, to remedy and prevent its impairment.

As a gesture towards international goodwill, ecological understanding, and peaceful use of the earth, Canada should donate one of its multitude of arctic islands to the United Nations, possibly at the time of the World Conference on the Human Environment. This island, which would be the first world park, might become an international centre for polar ecological research. Prime Minister Trudeau, who has frequently expressed the grave concern of his government on the question of protesting the arctic environment, should establish a task force to investigate and recommend a suitable site for the world park. One of the larger islands, such as Bathurst, Devon, or Somerset, might prove to contain representative plants, animals and landforms.

One of the most troublesome questions about wilderness areas and national parks is: how does one measure the value of such an area, in contrast with the value of the same area if used for other purposes? The alternative-use value of the wilderness area (which may, in fact, be high or low) represents the cost to society of reserving the area as wilderness. The justification for wilderness does not rest primarily on the direct economic value to users, but on the benefit to non-users and the preservation of a certain type of value or experience or of vital ecosystems.

Which would you rather have—Niagara Falls or a uranium mine? A rhetorical question to be sure, but one that isn't easily answered, especially on a long-term basis. We know the current value of a pound of uranium and can make future projections. But what of Niagara Falls? It is valuable simply because it is there. Any attempt to quantify it is almost certainly bound to fail—and yet that combination of rock and water is one of the most valuable pieces of real estate in the world. "The time has come," says eco-statistician Luna B. Leopold, "to use numbers to talk about the landscape—to objectively describe the landscape itself, with a rating system that would place values on the esthetic and ecological features of the environment so that the resulting data could be used in planning and decision making processes."[10]

Such a system of "landscape aesthetics" could be employed as counter arguments to those presented by the would-be exploiters of an area and would probably be as relevant as much of the numerical hocus-pocus, usually referred to as "cost-benefit ratios," that they present.

The major, direct economic benefits that come from wilderness areas and national parks are the result of the "use" of such areas by tourists. "It is entirely possible the value to the country of the open space will exceed the value of the minerals in the polar region," according to Dr. Fred Roots, co-ordinator of the Polar Intercontinental Shelf Project.[11] Roots believes that the clean air and water and uncluttered landscapes of the north will attract an ever-increasing number of visitors from the polluted and urbanized south.

At first glance, it might seem that Roots is being very unrealistic, to say the least, but in Alberta, which has depended on royalty revenue from oil and gas for a major part of its budget, the Tourist Association thinks that by 1985 the amount brought in by tourists (about $250 now, $750 million in 1985) will surpass both the oil-gas industry and agriculture.

The Trudeau administration, like those of Diefenbaker and Pearson, still seems mesmerized by predictions of the fabulous wealth which will be created by the exploitation of the non-renewable resources–oil, gas and minerals. This single-minded approach has precluded serious consideration of other possible uses, or "non-uses" of the north. Both the Yukon and the Northwest Territories have programs to encourage tourism, but with small staffs and budgets, they are little more than token efforts. It should be mentioned that despite its limitations the "Travel-arctic" promotion of the Northwest Territories is an extremely imaginative one and should be strengthened and expanded.

You can fly to Europe, from say Toronto, for a little over $200 on a charter–but it costs over $500 to fly to Inuvik or Resolute, and there are almost no charter flights. This cost of travel is a major obstacle to expanding tourism in the north. If the government subsidizes mineral exploration ($2 million a year) and oil-gas exploration ($33 million in Panarctic Oils) why should it not subsidize the tourist industry, at least to the same extent as it does those hunting for minerals? Funds should be made available for the construction of facilities to subsidize air fares and to advertise northern travel.

Surely we can resolve the land-use conflicts in an area of one and one-half million square miles. After all, most of the exploitive, extractive industries currently exploring the north will ultimately need a very small percentage of the land for the mines, oil and gas wells, and the pipelines if and when they are developed. The most important task now is to see that unnecessary damage does not occur during this exploration phase. There are two main methods of accomplishing this: strict controls on exploration activity and the setting aside of large areas as wilderness and/or national parks. Despite the promises of

Ottawa it seems unlikely that there will be strict controls, at least in the foreseeable future. There are too many legal loopholes in the Arctic Land Use Regulations to make them effective, even if the government were serious about enforcing them.

"If we err, let us err by dedicating too much parkland." pleaded R. A. Hemstock, Arctic Co-ordinator of Imperial Oil Limited in a talk to the Royal Society of Canada.[12] Hemstock proposed that about five times the percentage of land set aside for national parks in the south should be considered as a starting point in the north. This would amount to about 75,000 square miles—about five per cent of the land north of 60.

One of the most important reasons for setting aside large wilderness areas is that it keeps future options open. As we begin to calculate the costs of restoring and rehabilitating the land, the lakes, the rivers and the air of southern Canada, the arguments for preserving vast regions in the north are strengthened. If we don't know what we are doing, and no national emergency forces us to develop the north, we should wait until we better understand how to work and live there.

It would not be unrealistic to suggest that at least twenty-five per cent of the north—375,000 square miles—should be set aside as wilderness, national parks, and ecological research reserves.

To most Canadians, the Arctic is far, foreign, frigid and forbidding. More of us have crossed the Atlantic than the sixtieth parallel; more have visited Rome than Resolute. A major effort to foster a tourist industry would change all this—with immeasurable benefits to northerners and to all Canadians.

"My father, you have spoken well; you have told me that Heaven is very beautiful; tell me now one more thing. Is it more beautiful than the country of the musk-ox in summer, where sometimes the mist blows over the lakes, and sometimes the water is blue and the loons cry very often?"

Saltatha,

Indian Guide to Warburton Pike

CHAPTER 6 / *Who Owns the Beautiful Land?*

All of the beautiful land originally belonged to the Eskimos and the Indians. Some of it still does. No treaties exist between the Eskimo people and the Government of Canada, and although the Indian people signed away most of their rights, titles and privileges, important treaty provisions are still unfulfilled. The question of the rights and land claims of the Original Peoples–Eskimo, Indian and Métis–remains unresolved, and might have important implications as the resources of the north are exploited.

The current rush to exploit northern resources has touched off a wave of concern among the Original Peoples, and new leaders are emerging. They are educated, eloquent, and determined to seek a solution once and for all to their claims to the land.

Typical of these new leaders is Chief John Tetlichi, a member of the Council of the Northwest Territories. Chief John, more than half-seriously, says that his people may claim Atkinson Point, where Imperial Oil made its discovery, and the right-of-way of the proposed pipeline down the Mackenzie River. "Our people signed a treaty fifty years ago," says Chief Tetlichi, "but the location of lands promised to us has never been decided."[1]

Tetlichi, Chief of the Fort McPherson Indian Band, is referring to Treaty 11, signed in 1921 by chiefs and headmen from Providence, Simpson, Wrigley, Norman, Good Hope, Arctic Red River, McPherson, Liard, and Rae. The treaty covers most of the west half of the Northwest Territories, an area of about 372,000 square miles including the oil-gas rich Mackenzie Delta and the shore of the Beaufort Sea, from the Yukon border to the Coppermine River, including, of course, Atkinson Point.

Treaty 11 guarantees that the Slave, Dogrib, Hare, Loucheux, and other Indians "shall have the right to pursue their usual vocations of hunting, trapping and fishing throughout the tract surrendered," and the government "agrees and undertakes to lay aside reserves for each band, the same not to exceed in all one square mile for each family of five, or in that proportion for larger or smaller families."

These reserves, as Chief Tetlichi says, were never established. However, in 1959 a Federal Commission was established to review both Treaty 11 and Treaty 8, which covers lands to the south and east of those in Treaty 11. Commissioner Walter H. Nelson found that in 1954 there were an estimated 4,502 Indians in the fifteen bands covered by the treaties. Under the provisions of Treaties 8 and 11 they were entitled to 576,016 acres of land. But the Commissioner recommended that reserves not be set aside and that some other solution should be found. This was based on the Commission's finding that the Indians "do not want to live on reserves." Also, at that time, the Indians were not too interested in obtaining mineral rights; traditional rights (hunting, trapping, fishing) were of prime importance. Nevertheless, the Nelson Commission recommended payment of $20 for each of the 576,016 acres to which the Indians were entitled–a total of $11,520,320. The Nelson Commission also recommended "an annual payment of one per centum of any revenues derived by the Crown from the mineral, gas and oil resources of that part of the Northwest Territories described in Treaties 8 and 11."[2]

Dr. Roger Pearson of the University of Illinois, in a socio-economic study of the Great Slave Lake region, reported that by 1968 "there had been a considerable shift in opinions on the part of Indians regarding mineral rights claims."[3] For example, in a brief to the federal government, the Fort Smith Band proposed that

> compensation for ceding our land should be worked out by preparing an estimation of all resources harvested and mined within the boundaries of Treaties 8 and 11 and placing a value on these resources (that went to benefit whitemen in the south) and working out a formula which would be compensation for the Indian people . . . (estimated to be ½ of 1% or $75 million dollars) from the day Treaties 8 and 11 were signed to this day and date.[4]

The brief also suggested that Métis should be allowed to benefit from a land settlement and that once past claims are settled all future resource revenues should be turned over to the Government of the Northwest Territories.

An Indian Claims Commissioner, Professor Lloyd Barber, vice-president (administration) of the University of Saskatchewan, was appointed in December 1969 by the federal government. It will be his responsibility "in consultation with representatives of the Indians" to "inquire into and report upon how claims arising in respect of the performance of the terms of treaties and agreements formally entered into by representatives of the Indians and the Crown . . . may be adjudicated."[5]

The President of the Indian Brotherhood of the Northwest Territories, Roy Daniels, points out that "negotiations and submissions in reference to such claims (Treaties 8 and 11) will take time to make. . . ."[6] But time is running out in much of the area covered by the treaties. Permits to explore for oil and gas have been issued and many mineral claims have been staked.

Imperial Oil found oil at Atkinson Point, Amoco Petroleum is developing large gas reserves in the southwestern part of the treaty area, and several new mines are being planned. In the area around the east arm of Great Slave Lake, a national park will soon be developed.

On March 9, 1970, the Indian Brotherhood of the Northwest Territories presented a statement to the Minister of Indian Affairs and Northern Development in which they requested:

> that no further step be taken towards setting aside any lands in the areas of Treaties 8 and 11 for parks or for other special or restricted purposes which would affect adversely the continued exercise of our traditional rights, until we have had a fair and genuine opportunity to propose alternatives or to decide if we accept the park, if that is in the best interests of the Indian peoples of the Northwest Territories."[7]

In Alaska, a similar request by the Alaska Federation of Natives resulted in the Secretary of the Interior, then Stewart Udall, imposing a two-year "freeze" on further disposition of public lands.

The Indian people are concerned, not only about the park, but also the proposed pipeline which may run along the Mackenzie River. They fear the pipeline (48-inch diameter pipe) might block and disrupt the migration and movements of caribou–still the basic, or at least supplementary, food supply for many families.

"Two centuries before Christ, and perhaps even earlier," wrote the late Diamond Jenness, "the ancestors of the people we know today as Eskimos wandered unchallenged along the shores of the Canadian Arctic and roamed the tundra beyond the limit of trees."[8] But today they have no recognized rights and claims on "their" land. Curiously, the government does recognize their sole right to hunt and kill polar bears.

Apparently the only land claims they may have are under what is termed aboriginal rights. Prime Minister Trudeau bluntly says that his government "won't recognize aboriginal rights."[9] His remarks, however, were with respect to the rights of the Indian people, with whom the Government has many treaties and agreements. An Eskimo leader from Frobisher Bay asks, "what part of the land belongs to the Government of Canada?" He believes that "the Inukshuk [stone markers] are important . . . they claim the land." Simonie, the elected representative for the Eastern Arctic to the Council of the Northwest Territories recently told his fellow Councillors that the Eskimo will "have a lot to say about the land in the Northwest Territories. We have been here before anyone else."[10]

The Eskimo people of the Arctic held their first conference from July 13 to 20, 1970, at Coppermine in the Northwest Territories. Eskimo leaders from twenty-two communities throughout the Arctic–from Churchill in the south to Grise Fiord in the north, from Banks Island in the west to Repulse Bay in the east–were in attendance. It was the first opportunity for the Eskimo people to discuss their rights and land claims in the context of present and proposed policies and programs of the Government.

"The discussion at the conference clearly indicated the incompetence and indifference of the Department of Northern Development (charged by statute with looking after the welfare of the Eskimo people) in administering the affairs of the native people of the North," reported Professor Peter A. Cumming, associate dean at Osgoode Hall Law School, York University, who attended the Coppermine Conference as legal adviser to the Eskimo people.[11]

The Coppermine Conference passed a number of resolutions, and perhaps the most important was Resolution No. 1, which reads as follows:

> The Eskimo people of Sachs Harbour, Banks Island, unanimously and strongly object to any oil or gas exploration on Banks Island. Your government has issued leases for such exploration without any prior consultation whatsoever with the Eskimo people. These

actions are an example of your government's continuing complete disregard for the rights of the Eskimo people and are contrary to the standards of common human decency.

The Eskimo people of Banks Island are self-sufficient trappers and hunters, annually achieving the world's richest white fox harvest and have used these lands since time immemorial.

Banks Island has a very delicate ecological balance which will be destroyed if exploration is allowed and the land surface disturbed, as your government will readily understand if it will only choose to consult with the Eskimo people and have biologists conduct the necessary research. In contrast to the actions of your government, the Eskimo people have always practiced self imposed rigorous conservation measures to maintain the ecology of Banks Island. The Eskimo people cannot understand why your government has authorized such exploration when you continually profess to have concern for the environment of the North.

The people of Sachs Harbour urgently request that you direct that no further exploration take place until consultation can be made with the Eskimo people in these matters. Your government's failure to do so can only be interpreted as conscious consent to the destruction of the people of Sachs Harbour.

All of the Eskimo people of the North, as evidenced by the representatives' signatures, hereto completely support the people of Sachs Harbour in this urgent plea to you.

We also request that your government always have prior consultation with the Eskimo people in respect to any service, exploration or any other activities intended to be undertaken.

We also ask that your government recognize our rights as aboriginals in the lands of the North and give us fair compensation where there is expropriation of our rights in the lands. We believe that the Native people of the North should receive directly a fair share of the resources of the North similar to the proposed settlement being contemplated by the United States Government for the Native people of Alaska.[12]

This resolution, dealing with a matter of utmost urgency, was transmitted to the Prime Minister and the Minister of Indian Affairs and Northern Development by telegram. It was signed by Peter Esau and Peter Sidney, both of Sachs Harbour, with supporting signatures from twenty-two Eskimo communities.

Before we examine the official response, let us look at the events which precipitated this action.

The community of Sachs Harbour is virtually the only self-supporting, economically viable Eskimo community in the north. The 127 residents are trappers and hunters, with the richest white fox harvest in the world and an adequate supply of caribou, muskox, seal, geese and polar bear. There are only two families on welfare in the entire community—in both cases widows with children.

On June 25, 1970, a plane with nine hard-nosed oil men aboard landed at Sachs Harbour. They told the Eskimo people that a supply depot to supply oil operations in the western Arctic would be built on the island, with construction to start in August. They also said that extensive oil and gas exploration, including seismic blasting, would begin about December. This exploration might last three to five years.

Peter Esau told Professor Peter Cumming that the oil men offered the Eskimo people twenty labouring jobs while the supply depot was being constructed, at $1.67 per hour. Mr. Esau said that the oil men warned the Eskimos that they should not publicize the matter and refused to put any assurances in writing that their activities would not harm the island's ecology. Needless to say, there had been no consultation with the people of Sachs Harbour by the Department of Indian Affairs and Northern Development, who had issued 308 permits for exploration on the island.

Fortunately, the story was picked up by the southern press, with such headlines as BARBAROUS IS THE ONLY WORD on a *Globe and Mail* editorial dated August 5, 1970. The government was forced to take some action. On August 17, 1970, Northern Development Minister Chrétien visited Sachs Harbour and *Globe* reporter Lewis Seale was along. According to Mr. Seale, "Mr. Chrétien tried to reassure the Eskimos, not very successfully, and replied, when one Eskimo woman asked him, 'What will become of this island?', 'We don't know.' "[13]

However, on October 2, 1970, a typical Chrétien "all-is-well" communiqué was issued by the Department of Indian Affairs and Northern Development. The Minister says that he "asked officials of his Department to consult with the Banks Island Trappers Association, the oil companies, the Territorial Government and the Canadian Wildlife Service and prepare a set of strict operating regulations to prevent serious impairment to the ground surface of the island or to the local white fox and migratory bird populations. Copies of the regulations have been sent to the Trappers Association and to their legal representative and have been agreed to by both."[14]

Do the Eskimo people of Sachs Harbour have any choice? What if they rejected the government regulations? What recourse if any, do they have to the law? Might they find themselves moved farther south (or farther north) for health or other reasons?

The Eskimos of Sachs Harbour stand to lose, whether or not oil and gas are found under their trapping and hunting grounds. Despite government assurances, there is still the possibility of disturbance to the environment and wildlife; and if oil and gas are found the ensuing development will almost certainly cause changes. The Eskimo people can really only lose, for under the present policies of the Trudeau Government they won't share in any revenue generated from the resources on their land, and they will lose their present means of support.

The plight of the Eskimo people of Sachs Harbour symbolizes the dilemma facing most of the Original People of the North. They languish in limbo. Their traditional way of life is long lost, but most are unable to join the mainstream of our society. The Eskimo people aren't even sure of their identity: under the British North America Act, Eskimos are considered Indians —but they are not judged Indians under the Indian Act.

Mr. Chrétien blithely talks of the north as "an untouched desert, a wasteland, that appeared to have little value for Canada and Canadians. . . . We see now how wrong this view was," he continues, "for we now know that the North holds potential wealth of great value for all Canadians, northern and southern, alike."[15]

This "wasteland" was and is the home of the Eskimo people. And their homeland is threatened with destruction by the government's policies and programs to "Exploitarctic." With a rare sense of detachment, Mr. Chrétien says "it will take reasonable men seeking reasonable agreements to avoid potential conflicts."[16] Is the government reasonable in issuing permits for exploration, without prior study, that might seriously impair the Sachs Harbour people's source of support? Is the government reasonable in refusing to recognize aboriginal rights? Chrétien appears to be appealing to the rank greed of all Canadians, hoping they will forget the rights of the Orginal People in the scramble for riches.

Under the 1960 Canadian Bill of Rights (part 1, section 1), "it is . . . recognized and declared that in Canada there have existed and shall continue to exist without discrimination by reason of race, national origin, colour, religion or sex, the following human rights and fundamental freedoms, namely, (a) the right of the individual to life, liberty, security of the person, and enjoyment of property, and the right not to be deprived thereof except by due process of law;"[17]

"All people may, for their own ends, freely dispose of their wealth and resources," proclaims the International Covenant on Civil and Political Rights. "In no case may a people be deprived of its own subsistence."[18]

The principle of aboriginal rights has never been established in Canada. In good part this has been the fault of the Original People, who did not push their claims through the courts. Now this is changing. The Nishga Indian Nation is claiming aboriginal title to over 1,000 square miles of land in northwest British Columbia. The Nishga Nation has not entered into treaties or agreements with the Crown, the Hudson's Bay Company, or any other party. The Nishga Nation claims it holds rights and title

94

to the land by virtue of the Royal Proclamation of George III, issued on October 7, 1763, and because the Nishga have lived on the land "from time immemorial." They are now taking their case to the Supreme Court of Canada. Both a lower court and the British Columbia Court of Appeal have ruled that "if the nation ever enjoyed aboriginal rights or title to the land, they had lawfully been voided by 1871 when the province joined Confederation."[19] To a layman untutored in the ways of the law, this seems a *non-sequitur*.

A Yellowknife lawyer, Brian Purdy, has sought leave to intervene in the case, arguing that the decision of the B.C. Courts would materially affect the aboriginal rights and land claims of the Committee for Original People's Entitlements (COPE), which he represents. This committee was formed to "provide a united voice for all original peoples of the N.W.T." and to "work for the establishment and the realization of the rights of the original peoples." COPE's constitution defines an original person as "an Indian or Eskimo or the wife, husband, child, grandchild, or great-grandchild of an Indian or Eskimo, or the wife or husband of such a child, grandchild or great-grandchild."[20] The Canadian Woman of the Year in 1967, Mrs. Agnes Semmler, a Métis from Inuvik, is COPE's first president. An Eskimo, Victor Allan, and James Koe, an Indian, are the vice-presidents.

One of COPE's first actions was to retain the services of Brian Purdy. He was asked to investigate all legal aspects of their claims and rights and advise on what, if any legal action might be taken. Purdy has undertaken, with the help of law students in the south, a review of the whole question of rights–constitutional, treaty and aboriginal–not only in Canada, but in other parts of the world.

Purdy thinks that "Canada should make a deal now. A once-and-for-all payment would be morally, legally and financially in the best interests of all concerned."[21] Canada now spends about $350 million each year on foreign aid and it has been suggested, unofficially, that this might be the sort of settlement COPE will ask for. To put some perspective on things, Dr. W. H. Woodward, of the Department of Indian Affairs and Northern Development, says that royalties from arctic oil could amount to as much as $8 billion.

The United States Congress has just recently officially recognized the aboriginal rights of the native peoples of Alaska, and has passed legislation to include the recognition and setting aside of lands occupied by the natives (homes, businesses, and the like); setting aside of other lands near the settlements for hunting, fishing, trapping; compensation for lands taken in the past. The plan is to pay $100 million into a fund to be shared by all natives and to be administered by a new investment corporation; and compensation for all remaining aboriginal rights in the lands, probably a further payment or payments (possibly a percentage of royalties) to the investment fund.

This investment corporation (the proposed name is the Alaska Native Development Corporation) would be authorized to have one million shares of common stock and to issue shares equal to ten times the number of natives enrolled on the date of incorporation. Such stock will carry voting rights and be eligible for dividends. The Corporation may invest its funds, provide for the lending of funds to promote the economic development of the natives, provide loans for the education of individual natives, provide loans for charitable grants in time of distress, and provide loans for housing and other buildings.

Justice Arthur J. Goldberg, former Justice of the U.S. Supreme Court and U.S. Ambassador to the United Nations, who represented the Alaska Federation of Natives, summed up the situation:

> The settlement must make the Natives masters of their own destiny. They must determine the manner in which the settlement proceeds are to be invested and utilized. As a result of the settlement, each Native should be in a position to determine whether to continue with the traditional way of life, to join the mainstream of

American society, or to find some middle ground. No matter which way of life a Native may choose, the settlement must help to make that way of life a meaningful and satisfying one.[22]

The events in Alaska that led up to the U.S. Congressional recognition of aboriginal rights bear a striking similarity to those in Canada's north: primarily, a sudden surge to exploit the natural resources. If the Original Peoples are able to establish the principle of aboriginal rights, it could have a tremendous impact on the pattern and pace of northern economic development. COPE's president Agnes Semmler says that COPE is not seeking to stop this development; the Original Peoples simply want a just share.

The Coppermine Conference of Eskimo People concluded, according to Professor Peter Cumming, with a question:

> Will public opinion in Canada support the native people of the North and force the Federal Government to provide a fair and sensible solution to the problems caused to the people through exploration which is almost solely for the benefit of Canadians of the South?[23]

Canada should make every effort to resolve the question of aboriginal rights and to determine if some of the beautiful land still belongs to the Eskimo, the Indian and the Métis. Events in the north threaten the lands and livelihood of these people as never before. The problem can no longer be swept under the rug for some future Parliament; nor can it be left to interminable litigation. If there is no justice for Canada's first citizens, what hope is there for a Just Society?

"There are four interconnected threats to the planet–wars of mass destruction, overpopulation, pollution and depletion of resources. The basis of all four probems is the inadequacy of the sovereign states to manage the affairs of mankind in the twentieth century."

Prof. Richard A· Falk,

Center for Advanced Study in the Behavioral Sciences, Princeton University

Man is totally linked to the land. Even technological man is dependent on it, though for the most part he has lost contact with it. Technological man has become a major geological force, dramatically and drastically changing the face of the earth. He telescopes time–thinking in terms of milliseconds, while nature operates in millennia. And he is introducing an ever increasing number of synthetic and complex chemical compounds to the biosphere, with little or no knowledge of what their ecological effects may be.

Environmental pollution is a global affair. The catalogue of ecological catastrophies is growing at an alarming rate–air pollution, multiple hazards of widespread use of pesticides, pollution of water by urban and industrial wastes, radiation hazards from fallout and nuclear power plants, mercury, PCB's, biological backlash from such projects as the Aswan Dam . . . no continent or country escapes, and the bad news continues to come in.

The Arctic has taken on a new significance and is of increasing interest and importance. Its brumal barrens are among the last unspoiled and undeveloped areas on the face of the earth. As such they are of inestimable value–to science, as a vital outdoor laboratory, where the secrets of the biosphere may be hidden; to industry, as a source of raw resources; and to man, as a "remote control" on civilization and as a place to get away from fellow man.

The Arctic offers a last opportunity to establish a rational relationship with nature: developing without destroying. Fortunately for Canada and the world, one individual with a passion for privacy has recognized this:

> Canada regards herself as the trustee for all mankind for the peculiar ecological balance that now exists so precariously in the water, ice and land areas of the Arctic archipelago.
>
> We do not doubt for a moment that the rest of the world would find us at fault, and hold us liable, should we fail to ensure adequate protection of that environment from pollution or artificial deterioration. Canada will not permit this to happen.[1]

The speaker was Pierre Elliott Trudeau, Canada's fifteenth Prime Minister and the place, the House of Commons on October 24, 1969. The Honourable Members in the Chamber that day were present at the birth of a tenet for man's continuing survival in a rapidly changing world: the Trudeau Doctrine.

In the months following Mr. Trudeau explained and expanded the doctrine in speeches, meetings, interviews and legislation. He visited the United Nations in early November to discuss his government's plans to protect the arctic environment with U.N. Secretary-General U Thant. An important aspect of their meeting was a discussion of the need for international co-operation in pollution control, especially in the oceans. Prime Minister Trudeau reiterated Canada's responsibility "to all mankind to preserve the very delicate ecological balance of the area."

On April 15, 1970, Mr. Trudeau presented a detailed case for his government's actions in a speech to the annual meeting

100

of the Canadian Press in Toronto. First, he outlined some basic reasons for protecting environmental quality:

> If part of our heritage is wilderness, and if the measure of Canada is the quality of life available to Canadians, then we must act should there be any threat to either. We must act to protect the freshness of our air; we must act to protect the purity of our water; to conserve our living resources. If necessary, we must offer leadership to the world in these respects and withstand the cries of complaining interests.

He went on to describe the significance of the Arctic as a "remote-control" on civilization:

> The Arctic ice pack has been described as the most significant surface area of the globe, for it controls the temperature of much of the Northern Hemisphere. Its continued existence in unspoiled form is vital to all mankind. The single most imminent threat to the Arctic at this time is threat of a large oil spill. . . . oil would spread immediately beneath ice many feet thick; it would congeal and block the breathing holes of the peculiar species of mammals that frequent the region: It would destroy effectively the primary source of food for Eskimos and carnivorous wildlife throughout an area of thousands of square miles; it would foul and destroy the only known nesting area of several species of wild birds. Because of the minute rate of hydrocarbon decomposition in frigid areas, the presence of any such oil must be regarded as permanent. The disastrous consequences which the presence would have on marine plankton, upon the process of oxygenation in the Arctic, and upon other natural and vital processes of the biosphere, are incalculable in their extent.

Lastly, Mr. Trudeau detailed the Arctic's vital importance to mankind's very survival:

> Involved here, in short, are issues which even the most conservative of environmental scientists do not hesitate to describe as being of a magnitude which is capable of affecting the quality, and perhaps the continued existence, of human and animal life

in the vast regions of North America and elsewhere. These are issues of such immense importance that they demand prompt and effective action. But this huge area cannot be protected by Canada alone. Just as the Arctic environment is of benefit to many nations, so only, in the long run, will international controls be able to effectively protect it."

Prime Minister Trudeau is saying that the Arctic is not only of great economic value, but of vital ecological importance to Canada and the world; he is saying that Canada invites international co-operation, but is prepared to act alone to protect and preserve the Arctic environment; and he is saying that Canada will offer leadership in the struggle to ensure man's survival in a changing and rapidly deteriorating world.

A start was made, on February 16, 1970, in translating the doctrine into the law of the land. Bill C-187, *An Act respecting inland water resources in the Yukon Territory and Northwest Territories,* was introduced by the Minister of Indian Affairs and Northern Development to the second session of the 28th Parliament. Under Bill C-187, the ". . . inland waters in the North will remain for all time public property to be used, managed and developed in the interest of the region and the nation as a whole." This was followed on April 8, 1970, by Bill C-202, *An Act to prevent pollution of the areas of the arctic waters adjacent to the mainland and the islands of the Canadian arctic.*" Bill C-202 was to be described by the Prime Minister to be "as exciting and as imaginative a concept as this government has undertaken."[2] The Trudeau Doctrine is written into legislation for the first time:

> And whereas Parliament at the same time recognizes and is determined to fulfil its obligations to see that the natural resources of the Canadian arctic are developed and exploited and the arctic waters adjacent to the mainland and islands of the Canadian arctic are navigated only in a manner that takes cognizance of Canada's responsibility for the welfare of the Eskimo and other inhabitants of the Canadian arctic and the preservation of the peculiar eco-

logical balance that now exists in the water, ice and land areas of the Canadian arctic . . ."[3]

Finally, on May 11th, Bill C-212, *An Act to Amend the Yukon Act, the Northwest Territories Act and the Territorial Lands Act,* was brought forward. The pertinent sections of this bill are amendments to the Territorial Lands Act, which will allow the establishment of northern land use regulations and zoning of the entire Canadian north.

Although the three Acts are of considerable importance, they still represent a fragmented approach to the problems of preserving the integrity of the Arctic's ecological regime. There is a desperate need for action to recognize and establish a comprehensive, all-embracing environmental policy. Inherent in such a policy should be the premise that ecological principles and considerations are equal to, and as important as, economic ones. As John Milton of the Conservation Foundation states: "The development system has tended to look at single problems and ignore the multiple side effects that are brought about by the resultant changes in the environment."[4] Down north, man's laws must be based on an understanding of nature's rules.

The *Arctic Waters Pollution Prevention Act,* in extending Canada's pollution prevention zone to 100 miles from land, establishes what Prime Minister Trudeau refers to as our "territorial imperative" in that region. However, the Prime Minister realistically realizes that "in the long run only international agreements will be able to effectively protect it."[5] International agreements are fraught with dangers and difficulties, especially when of necessity they restrict movement, trade, or resource harvest. Some of the existing international conservation agreements, such as those on whaling and fisheries, have been broken time and time again. But with man's very survival possibly at stake, the world must continue to take new initiatives in seeking agreement on rational policies to control global pollution and establish standards of environmental quality.

A unique opportunity for imaginative proposals and new initiatives is the World Conference on the Human Environment to be held in Sweden in 1972. The Conference is being organized to stimulate international agreement and co-operation for action on what Secretary-General U Thant calls "the crisis of the human environment" that threatens the very "future of life on earth." The Secretary-General's report on the environment states that there is an "urgent" need to halt and reverse trends toward the pollution of air and water, overcrowding and deterioration of cities, improper and over-use of land, and the potential extinction of many forms of plant and animal life.[6] Canada has played a leading role both in proposing and in planning the Conference. And recently a noted Canadian, Maurice Strong, was named to direct the preparations of this all-important undertaking.

But what face will Canada and Mr. Trudeau present to the world? To date, most of her efforts dealing with the environment are half-measures, unworthy of a country seeking to lead world efforts. Canada's program to preserve "the peculiar ecological balance in the Arctic" is marred by duplicity and a reluctance to take bold but necessary action. Reflect for a moment on the words of the late Diamond Jenness:

> In the United Nations Canada has presented the image of a Knight Errant, a champion of undeveloped and oppressed peoples and a builder of international peace and goodwill; but within the Dominion, half-hidden from the world's view, she has shown a different face. There she has secluded most of her Indians on out-of-sight reservations and confined her Eskimos to the Arctic, refusing to invite either race to unite with her in developing the common homeland, but clinging irrationally to the pre-Darwinian myth of the white man's superiority.[7]

In the crucible of the world community, what answer does Canada give if South Africa asks why we deny our Eskimos their aboriginal rights to the land and its resources? What answer if India asks about our policy towards zero-population growth? What answer if Russia asks why we recently began sports hunting of the "threatened" polar bear? What answer if undeveloped countries ask why we do not devote at least one per cent of our gross national product to aid developing countries?

Mr. Trudeau's invitation to the international community "to join with us and support our initiative for a new concept, an international legal regime designed to ensure to human beings the right to live in a wholesome natural environment"[8] is of great importance and the utmost urgency. But his case would be immeasurably strengthened if he were able to point to strong Canadian policies and programs of environmental conservation and preservation and of efforts to promote co-operation among circumpolar nations for Arctic conservation.

The essence of the Trudeau Doctrine is that if we are to ensure man's survival on earth ecology must engulf economics and internationalism must supplant nationalism. The Prime Minister might well ask "if the Canadian people will support me."[9] It will take considerable innovation and intellectual daring on Mr. Trudeau's part to keep the doctrine's dreams of reason from being turned into nightmares of reality.

"I have no doubt whatever that the real petroleum elephant* of the western hemisphere is in the island and offshore areas of the Canadian Arctic. . . ."

Charles R. Hetherington,

President, Panarctic Oils Limited

CHAPTER 8 / *Stop the Elephant Hunt*

Canada should put "time-locks" on some of the vaults in her northern natural treasure house.

There are sound economic, ecological and social reasons why the government should stop the arctic elephant hunt–the search for billion-barrel pools of oil and vast reserves of natural gas. Stop the search for minerals–uranium, copper, nickel, lead, zinc, silver, iron and others. Call off technology, for the first time in history–until it can be shown that man and his machines are able to operate in the fragile northern environment without doing irreversible damage, the long-term consequences of which might far outweigh any short-term economic gains.

"There is no present need for [arctic] oil," asserts a leading expert on Canada's petroleum regime, Professor A. R. Thompson.[1] This opinion is shared somewhat by Energy Minister Joe Greene, who was quoted in *Oilweek*: "We have great reserves for Canadian needs. We have billions of dollars worth of oil in the tar sands."[2]

---

*"Elephant," in the language of the petroleum people, means large—i.e. billion barrel—pools of oil.

The Athabasca Tar Sands, in north-eastern Alberta, "contain bitumen equivalent to 370 billion barrels of recoverable oil, and are considered to be the largest known reservoir of oil in the world," according to the Department of Indian Affairs and Northern Development.[3] By comparison, the recent discovery at Alaska's Prudhoe Bay is estimated at about ten billion barrels, which may be doubled by further exploration. The Tar Sands hold enough oil to meet Canada's 1969 demand rate for 700 years and North America's for 100, wrote Earle Gray in *Impact of Oil*.[4] Even if the demand rate doubles by 1990 as predicted by the National Energy Board, the Sands hold at least a fifty-year North American supply.

"The presence of the oil sands has been known for nearly 200 years," wrote Robert McClements, Jr. "Their economic potential has been recognized for more than 75 years; a basic method of separating the bitumen from the sands has been known for more than 30 years. . . ."[5]

Inexplicably, the immense tar sands reserves are virtually ignored in the predictions and forecasts of oil supply and demand by the National Energy Board in a seemingly authoritative study, *Energy Supply and Demand in Canada and Export Demand for Canadian Energy: 1966 to 1990.*[6] This gives a "wonderland" aura to the whole question of oil reserves. It results in a false sense of urgency of the need to find and "prove-up" new reserves.

At present only one plant, that of the Great Canadian Oil Sands Limited at Fort McMurray, is extracting oil from the Sands. But at least two others are in the planning stage–a $195 million plant by Syncrude Canada Limited and a $1 billion undertaking by Japan Petroleum Development Corporation.

The Government of Alberta's Oil and Gas Conservation Board maintains rigid quotas on oil production from the Tar Sands. Doubtless, large-scale production would upset the complex and "protectionist" American petroleum marketing system.

There are other proven and potentially productive reserves in Canada–in Alberta (where production is limited), Saskatchewan, Hudson Bay and off the east and west coasts. The east coast seems to hold the most promise of viable discoveries in the near future. Shell Canada has encountered oil and/or gas shows in each of ten recent wildcat drill holes. And in June 1970, Shell Canada and its American affiliate entered into a $250 million exploration and development program–the bulk of the funds presumably going to the east coast operations. Although there are possible pollution problems in off-shore oil production, an east coast discovery would have the distinct advantage of being close to the major eastern seaboard market.

Other latent sources of vast quantities of petroleum are the oil shales in Colorado, estimated to contain up to 1,000 billion barrels of oil, and the tremendous coal reserves of Canada and the United States, estimated to be over three trillion tons– equivalent in energy value to some 14 trillion barrels of oil. Studies by oil companies and the U.S. government indicate that gasoline and gaseous fuels may be produced from coal at costs not too much higher than that of gasoline from crude oil, according to Earle Gray.

Thus it seems reasonable to assume that there should not be any shortage of petroleum for some time into the future. There could be a much greater "lead" time, for exploitation of arctic oil, than is suggested by industry and government alike.

What of the economic benefits to the people of Canada of this activity to date? By the end of April 1970, the federal government had issued about 9,450 permits and 445 leases on 456.7 million acres in the Northwest Territories and the Yukon. In this region, about 300 million acres may be considered to be potentially productive of oil and gas, according to the Department of Indian Affairs and Northern Development. Only about $60 million has been received for these permits and leases– for an area larger than all but fourteen of the world's countries.

By comparison, Alberta took in $119.5 million for oil and gas rights in 1969 on only 5 million acres.

Is there a short-term need for additional mineral exploration and exploitation north of 60? "There are mineral resources there," wrote Professor Jim Lotz in *The Myth of the Rich North*, "but they are not the sort of resources that the world is short of, and they cannot be competitive in world markets without heavy government subsidy."[7] Northern mines currently produce gold, silver, asbestos, tungsten, copper and lead-zinc. There are proven reserves of billions of tons of iron ore, a hundred million tons of lead-zinc, and tens of millions of tons of copper and asbestos. But with the exception of tungsten there are large reserves in more accessible parts of Canada, of all minerals found thus far in the north. Almost all northern mines required initial government financial support and some continuing operating subsidies. Lotz asks, ". . . if the North is so rich why does the federal government have to put up $26,477,000 to assist in bringing a new lead-zinc mine into production in the Yukon?" Or, why is it considering investing $25,000,000 in a Baffin Island iron mine? Or, for that matter, why has it sunk $23.5 million into Panarctic Oils?

In the past few years staking "rushes" have taken place in several areas of the north. Major activity took place at Pine Point (27,000 claims), Coppermine (39,000 claims), Ross River-Anvil (10,000 claims), Artilery Lake (8500 claims), and the Dawson Range (13,000 claims). Anyone who has dabbled in penny mining stocks knows that many properties show promise but few produce. From 1966 to 1969, the federal government spent over $100 million on mine development alone. In addition, there are Northern Roads, Northern Mineral Exploration Assistance, Prospector's Assistance, and Northern Resource Airports Assistance Programs.

In June 1970, another $1 million was offered by the Federal Government to mining exploration companies under the Northern Mineral Exploration Assistance Program. In contrast, only

$500,000 was allotted to the Arctic Land Use Research Program. A revealing, but disturbing, insight into government priorities in the north.

Perhaps the government should allow the marketplace to decide when it is economically feasible to develop northern mineral resources. Should the government, at this time and using tax dollars, "assume a reasonable part of the risk" for the entrepreneurs it is inviting north? Or would this investment be put to better use in other "economically depressed" regions of Canada?

Imperial Oil Limited's Chairman, W. O. Twaits, believes that "within the next ten or fifteen years, 20 billion barrels [of oil] will be delineated" in Canada's Arctic.[8] At current Alberta prices, $2.60 per barrel of crude at wellhead, the twenty billion barrels would be worth $52 billion. Little wonder there is a rush to find the arctic elephants!

However, Mr. Twaits says "a major factor in this kind of development is the size of pre-investment before any cash return is realized." Pre-investment might require "in the order of $9.5 billion in finding and developing to a producible basis" and for transportation for oil and associated natural gas "an additional $3.5–$4 billion. . . . Thus we are looking at something like $13 billion if the North has some portion of the presently estimated potential." This compares rather closely with the total investment in southern, western Canada between 1947–69. A proposed natural gas pipeline from Prudhoe Bay to Edmonton may require a $1.5–$2 billion outlay.

There is no doubt that the economic aspects of northern oil and gas are somewhat staggering at first glance. Unfortunately it is not clear who will benefit if this development takes place. The Original Peoples?–Individually, perhaps, but they won't receive any share of royalties or rentals (although they may have legitimate claims to some of the land). The people of Canada?–thousands of man-years' employment will be created (for the most part jobs will require a high degree of technical skill and education); royalties will add to the federal treasury; and much of the production will possibly be sold to the United States. But the Canadian people must continue to support the various programs for the Original Peoples and probably bear much of the cost of pollution and rehabilitation.

"Canada has grievously fumbled in her Arctic," wrote the late Diamond Jenness in *Eskimo Administration: Analysis and Reflections,* "She has never faced the problems squarely, never set forth any clear statement of her aims in that region or co-ordinated her various programs to ensure their working in harmony."[9] Jenness was, of course, describing the plight of the Eskimos, but his remarks apply equally well to the present fragmented policies and programs for northern development.

"Exploitarctic!" appears to be the slogan of the Department of Indian Affairs and Northern Development. "The present approach to Canada's northern development is a frankly exploitive, looting operation that will enrich a few promoters (some of whom are non-Canadians) at the taxpayer's expense." claims Professor Jim Lotz.

Despite the national and world-wide concern about pollution and the deteriorating quality of the environment, the government has made no attempt to slow down exploration for oil, gas and minerals in the Arctic. On the contrary, they continue to boost it. As a government promotional pamphlet puts it: "Today, the combination of private enterprise and initiative with the full co-operation, encouragement and assistance of the Federal Government, is fashioning a chain of keys to unlock the great natural storage vaults containing Canada's resources."[10] Needless to say, there is not one word in the pamphlet concerning conservation—even though it was released in 1969.

The 200,000-member Canadian Wildlife Federation believes that there is an urgent need to slow the rate of northern exploration and damage, "until research and experimentation have produced techniques for coping with the special problems

112

of the North."[11] "The unseemly haste to press work in the Arctic seems hard to justify," says Clive E. Goodwin, executive director of the Conservation Council of Ontario, in announcing the Council's support of the CWF moratorium proposal.[12] Total membership of the organizations affiliated with the CCO totals over 900,000.

The Canadian Commission for UNESCO has called for a halt to arctic oil exploration until government research shows that there is a safe way to ship it out.

Dr. W. A. Fuller goes even further and questions "whether we should use Arctic oil at all." Fuller, acting head of the University of Alberta's Zoology Department, says: "There is a limit to the amount of hydrocarbon we can ultimately use; there is a lot more to be found buried or developed than we can ever use. . . . Because of the fragility of the environment, we should not even look for hydrocarbons in certain parts of the globe."[13]

A study by the United States National Academy of Sciences, *Resources and Man,* concluded that the "world supply of liquid hydrocarbons will only last another 100 years at the most and should be conserved for chemical purposes."[14]

"It would be in the best interests of all concerned, including the oil companies," says the Canadian Wildlife Federation, "for the government of Canada to take action to delay this sudden and uncontrolled acceleration in oil exploration." A partial moratorium, according to the CWF, would allow time for:

* Development of new techniques, or modifications of existing ones for exploration, development and production without extensive damage.
* Ecological research to establish the levels of disturbance which can be tolerated in the Arctic.
* Testing the feasibility of transport of oil through Arctic waters by tanker or submarine.
* Conducting research into the effects of oil spills, on land and at sea, under Arctic conditions; development of techniques for accomplishing the degree of clean-up indicated by that research.

* Development of stand-by facilities, equipment and staff necessary to ensure adequate clean-up in case of accidental oil spills.
* Studying the feasibility of permitting off-shore drilling under the conditions of ice, wind speed and temperature prevailing in the Arctic.
* Training the Indians and Eskimos in the skills used in all phases of exploration, development and production of oil so that the native people can play a significant role in helping to develop their country.[15]

"A practical man," said Disraeli, "is a man you can count upon to perpetuate the errors of his ancestors."

Down north, it is practical men who say: "Discover the first ventures into natural resource development that have been etched on the once silent landscape of forests, tundra, plain and mountains."[16] It is practical men who extol "the growling bulldozers carving airstrips and roads through tundra and forest, the towering drilling rigs marching north to the Arctic Ocean . . . opening new vistas on the Canadian landscape."[17]

The not-so-practical say "North . . . lies a different kind of land–too barren to ever be thickly settled, too bleak to be popular. . . . There is no doubt it will always be there, and so long as it is there Canada will not die."[18] And as another dreamer said, "It is to be hoped that there will never be so few caribou that it will be possible to count them."[19]

It was practical men who shattered the silence of southern forests and plains, disturbing and destroying, and left a legacy of broken landscapes and polluted water and air. Most of this took place before man realized what harm he was doing, and is regarded more in anguish than in anger. There is no excuse for this to happen down north: we have been warned. But will we take heed?

For a few moments, let's look at the north through impractical eyes. Let us suppose that the federal government declared all of Canada north of the 60th parallel a park–"Top of the World Park," if you like. Some vested interests, such as mining

114

and petroleum corporations, would undoubtedly object and point to their investments. But it might be in the long-term economic interests of the Canadian taxpayer to settle any claims they might have. Consider, for example, the estimate of the Canadian Council of Resource Ministers, that water pollution alone costs Canadians $1,172,900,000 each year; or Energy Minister Greene's suggested figure of $4 billion needed to clean up water pollution across the country (if it's like most government programs you can double or triple the amount). But if a wildcat well blew out of control in the Mackenzie Delta, the taxpayer would pay the major share of clean-up costs—which could run into tens of millions, not to mention incalculable permanent damage to the wildlife and environment.

Resource development would be allowed in this park; in fact it would be encouraged—but under new rules. Down north, entrepreneurs would have to present detailed plans of proposed developments, with the onus on them to prove to the satisfaction of a Council on Ecological and Economic Affairs that the project is economically viable (does not require substantial government support) and ecologically sound.

Thus the north would be developed gradually, on a rational basis—allowing only those developments that are in the public interest, and keeping out those designed primarily to enrich the entrepreneur, often at public expense. In effect, we would be allowing the marketplace, in concert with ecological reality, to determine the pace of resource development in almost half of Canada. Meanwhile, Canadians and Americans could enjoy a vast outdoor recreation area. If this were properly developed, the contribution to the economy might at least equal, if not exceed, any revenue from resource exploitation that residents of the north might receive.

The Government of Canada should declare a moratorium, partial or complete, on further resource exploration and exploitation in Canada north of the 60th parallel. The most vital reasons for a moratorium are:

115

1. The government is clearly not prepared for the current rush of exploration; immeasurable, irreversible environmental damage may result.
2. There is no apparent short-term need, as determined by the marketplace, for northern natural resources.
3. The rights of the Original Peoples (Eskimo, Indian and Métis) with respect to ownership of northern land and resources are in doubt and dispute.
4. There is a serious lack of basic knowledge of the Arctic and sub-Arctic ecosystems. Such knowledge is essential for a rational plan of conservation and development.
5. The Government of Canada does not have an overall, comprehensive long range plan for Northern Development.

A moratorium is essential if the forty per cent of Canada that lies north of 60 is to escape degradation and possible destruction by the untamed technology of our cybernetic, synthetic society. Unless the industrial incursion is brought to a full stop, expediency threatens to overwhelm ecological reality. The pattern so familiar in the south–of a "minor" concession here, a "necessary" exception there–is emerging down north, and before long compromise may become capitulation.

A moratorium would allow time for the development of long-range plans: for an ecological survey, for the settlement of the status of the Original Peoples and their rights, for the setting aside of adequate parks and scientific reserves, for the negotiation of fair taxes and royalties on resource production, for study of the best means of retaining Canadian ownership and control over northern resources, and for a Northern Environmental Policy Act. It would also allow time for an assessment of the effects, to date, of resource exploration and development, time for research to determine the parameters of the northern environment, and time to establish administrative and enforcement programs and personnel to control development.

In a major speech to the Senate on the "dangers to our en-

116

vironment" on October 14, 1969, Senator John Nichol warned that ". . . industrial expansion is not intrinsically good. It is good only as it helps mankind in a total sense. If it provides him with a job and a standard of living, and at the same time destroys the world in which he is going to live, it does not accomplish what it is setting out to do for man."[20]

A UNESCO report on "The Biosphere Conference" summarized a discussion on human ecology in the following words:

> Whether the challenges come from the physical or social forces, the diversity of environments is of crucial importance for the evolution of man and his societies because the ultimate result of a stereotyped and equalized environment can be and often is an impoverishment of life, a progressive loss of the qualities that we identify with humanness and a weakening of physical and mental health. Our policy should be to preserve or to create as many diversified environments as possible. Richness and diversity of physical and social environments constitute a crucial aspect of adaptions of functions to needs, whether in the planning of rural and urban areas, the design of dwellings or the management of individual life.[21]

The concern of conservation is not just for birds and bees and beavers, but for people; the concern is not just for changes in life-style, but for the challenges to life itself. The "Battle for the Biosphere" is not just a fight to save whooping cranes and whales, but a struggle to save man and to ensure the continuance of life as we know it.

Prime Minister Trudeau believes that "these are issues of such immense importance that they demand prompt and effective action," and that his government must "withstand the cries of complaining interests"[22]–interests, one might add, like the petroleum industry, with spokesmen such as the chairman of Imperial Oil Limited, W. O. Twaits, who told his shareholders recently that "if developments in these areas [the Arctic] are to be viable–if their great potential contributions to the Canadian nation are to be realized–the competitive handicaps resulting from the environment in which they will be undertaken must be minimized. They simply cannot carry unduly heavy burdens of regulation and taxation."[23] Or interests such as the mining industry, which has consistently but discreetly opposed parks and reserves in the north, with spokesmen like L. C. Morrisroe, president of Cadillac Explorations Limited, who defined his company's mineral interest (which conflicts with a potential park on the South Nahanni River) as follows: "We're not really all that interested in the scenery and the animals. What we want to do is to make some money out of it."[24]

Senator John Nichol says, "the overall ecological problem will not be solved without some major economic dislocations, at least in the short term. . . . We need new rules."[25] The time for these new rules is now. The place is down north. For if the oft-repeated concern for the future well-being of our children and our children's children is ever to be more than just a sepulchral cliché, we must sometime, somewhere, make a start toward new values and priorities for our society.

We cannot plead ignorance or the inability to pay. The ecological explosion of 1969, while catching politicians, the public, and many scientists by surprise, exposed in devastating detail the dangers man faces if he continues his arrogant attitude towards the environment. If Canada–an industrialized and affluent country with a high, material standard of living and natural resources far in excess of immediate needs–cannot "afford" to slow down development in one of its frontier areas, what country on earth can?

If the vision is the environment, if the vision is man's welfare and well-being, then we have no alternative but to stop the elephant hunt.

"Where there is no vision, the people perish."

Proverbs, 29:18.

CHAPTER 9 / *If the Environment is the Vision*

There are serious doubts as to whether, at least in ecological terms, man and his machines should be in the Arctic at all. During the past five years, man has had more impact and wrought more changes on the fragile face of the north than at any time since life on earth began several hundred million years ago. The reverence for life and land of the Indian and Eskimo has been replaced by the arrogance of the technocrat and engineer.

The Eskimo was, and still is in some scattered communities, an integral part of the ecosystem. The Eskimo lived off the land, taking his energy from the surplus of the annual fixation of biological energy. And his numbers were, to a great extent, regulated by the vagaries of nature. The technological-industrial invaders of the Arctic–who, ironically, come seeking "buried energy"–do not depend on available energy; they import their supply. This is done at enormous expense, both economic and ecologic, and tends to isolate and detach modern man in the north from the harsh realities of nature.

This is made possible by technology, which has been described as the "systematic application of scientific and other organized knowledge to practical tasks."[1] While we should not underestimate the benefits bestowed on mankind by technology, we should not overestimate the capacity of technology to undertake successfully any and every task. Man is just beginning to realize that some schemes, such as the supersonic aircraft, which may be feasible technologically, would be folly ecologically. There must be a re-appraisal of what is practical in the light of new insights into the complexities of the global environment.

Technology has been tried in the Arctic and found wanting. Already two wildcat wells have blown out of control on remote islands, and two large barges, one loaded with fuel, have been crushed by the ice. The mighty *Manhattan* returned with gaping holes. At this point in time, considering our relatively unsophisticated terrestrial technology, should we be contemplating large-scale northern development and settlement? In terms of energy consumption–no. Man would get less production for every unit of energy invested in the north, according to Dr. W. Fuller, than if he were to invest the same amount of energy in Toronto or Boston or Vancouver. For much of the year, the environmental conditions–cold and darkness–are extremely inhospitable. So what is actually taking place is a massive search for non-renewable resources (oil, natural gas, minerals) which may be pumped or shipped south. Greed, not need (at least not Canadian need), has been the major force behind this black gold rush. For to this date there is no resource north of the sixtieth parallel which is currently in short supply in Canada, or likely to be in the near future.

The north is still a quality environment, one of the few large expanses of relatively unspoiled landscape left on earth. Before it is too late, Canadians should question the need to drill thousands of so-called discovery wells across the Arctic–each of which is a potential ecological disaster of unknown dimensions. They should question the necessity of exploding countless thousands of charges of dynamite just to locate possible drilling sites. The time has come to turn technology around and bring it under control.

Until recently, society has regarded events such as well blow-outs, dynamite blasts killing wildlife, and bulldozers damaging the landscape, as "side-effects." They were regrettable, but incidental to the important task at hand. Ecologists and conservationists challenge this concept. They believe that we must "take note of *all* costs and *all* benefits, so there will be no 'effects' that are 'side'. The analysis and decision process can then 'internalize the externalities', be truly comprehensive in identifying the trade-offs, identify who is actually paying, or not paying, whom, for what, in the proposed action."[2]

Canadian politicians and bureaucrats tend to believe that the answer to environmental problems caused by technology is simply more technology. They continue to place blind faith in technology's ability to solve ecological problems–while in fact some of the problems cannot be "solved." As ecologist Barry Commoner wrote in *Science and Survival,* "The age of innocent faith in science and technology may be over."[3] The ecologist must provide positive alternatives, not just dispel this innocent faith.

The basic task of ecology is not to tinker with technology, but to create an awareness and understanding among policy-makers of the vital necessity to slow down the rush towards environmental disaster and the progressive destruction of the earth's irreplacable resources. This concept of making more rational use of the earth's resources is often referred to as conservation. Some confusion exists as to the relationship between ecology and conservation–but basically, ecology is a science, conservation an art; ecology supplies the facts, conservation the philosophy.

Conservation has sometimes been likened to prohibition by cynical critics who delighted in deriding the "dickie-bird watchers", the "do-gooders," the "old ladies of both sexes." In the past, this is somewhat understandable, because conservationists have often come to public attention because they were opposed to some grand design to dam a wild river, cut sawlogs in a wilderness park, or drain and fill in a marsh. They were said to be against that nebulous thing, "progress." Their battle cry was "preserve or perish!" and they were mainly engaged in efforts to save wild nature–something which is still of great importance.

Now that has all changed. Conservationists such as Raymond Dasmann suggest that we must strive to maintain diversity in both natural and man-made environments if we are to provide the greatest possible variety and the highest quality of living for mankind.

This question of environmental quality has never received any serious consideration in Canada. A recent report of the Science Council of Canada on goals for science fails to mention environmental quality as one of the six major goals. The World Health Organization says that environmental quality is adequate when: the health of even sensitive sectors of the population would not be adversely affected; concentrations of pollutants do not cause an annoyance, such as unpleasant odours or taste; natural scenery is not obscured; damage to domestic and wild animals, ornamental plants, forests, and crops would not occur; fabrics would not be soiled, deteriorated, or their colours affected; metals would not be corroded and other materials would not be damaged; and visibility would not be significantly reduced.

While the problems of the environment are exceedingly complex, a relatively simple safeguard has been suggested which if implemented would greatly reduce environmental damage. The rule is: "Disturbance of any natural environment should not exceed the minimum needed to accomplish its rational use for worthy human goals."[4]

Unfortunately, this would be difficult, if not impossible, to do in our north. Under the present system, one cabinet minister, the Minister of Indian Affairs and Northern Development, is responsible both for promoting northern economic exploitation and for safeguarding the environment–an impossible task for any man. The newly created Department of the Environment is not going to administer the only significant part of Canada's environment over which the federal government has complete control. The acts which deal with northern conservation–Arctic Waters Pollution Prevention Act, the Northern Inland Waters Act and the Territorial Lands Act–remain under the Minister of Indian Affairs and Northern Development.

In order to safeguard the environment of the north and put economic exploitation in proper perspective, the Department of Indian Affairs and Northern Development should be abolished and its various responsibilities transferred to other departments, as follows:

1. Indian Affairs–to the Department of the Secretary of State.
2. Northern Development–to the Department of Regional Economic Expansion.
3. Conservation–to the Department of the Environment.

Mere administrative juggling does not solve long-standing problems, but at least there will be a fresh, and hopefully more enlightened approach to the problems of the north, its peoples and its environment, if more than one minister and one bureaucracy is involved. The Indians and Eskimos deserve to share in any wealth found in the north,–but they are not likely to under the present set-up, which is preoccupied with encouraging entrepreneurs to exploit the non-renewable resources. Putting northern development in the Department of Regional Economic Expansion means that programs for the north will have to compete for funds with those of long-settled and economically depressed regions of the country. It seems obvious that it is not good business to have one man saying on the one hand "Come and seek the riches of the north," and on the other, "We have strict operating rules up here."

It is a major function of Parliament to propose and consider policies to provide for the health, welfare and well-being of the people of Canada. A challenge to the safety and welfare of Canada and the Canadian people has arisen. The challenge is the rapid deterioration of the environment, which is the indispensable foundation of Canadian prosperity, security and welfare.

There seems to be no end to the bad news—the demise of Lake Erie, DDT, phosphates in detergents, pesticides in polar bears and penguins, and mercury. There is now sufficient scientific evidence to establish that the threats to the environment and to man are real and growing worse—there is, in fact, an ecological crisis.

The federal government has reacted to this crisis in the environment by a series of half-measures, hastily taken and sometimes based on inadequate or faulty information. Let us take the example of phosphates in detergents. For many years there have been reports of massive blooms of algae in Lake Erie—the lake, in fact, was said to be "dying." It was suggested that phosphates found in high concentrations in the detergents used for the family wash were the crucial nutrient that determined the size of the algal blooms. That is plausible, but unproved.

Then a bright group of students at the University of Toronto analyzed all the leading detergents and published their findings —which showed that many brands contained as much as forty per cent phosphate. The media took up the story and gave it wide publicity. Shortly afterward, Minister of Energy and Resources Joe Greene announced that the government would require manufacturers to reduce drastically the phosphate content of detergents by 1972.

The drive to virtually eliminate phosphates from detergents may not solve the problem of algal blooms for there are many other sources of these chemicals in industrial, municipal and agricultural wastes. A more satisfactory solution might be more sophisticated waste treatment and reduced use of synthetic fertilizer. But even this is not certain.

125

The main point is that the government, confronted by a handful of bright, informed and determined Pollution Probers, panicked. Why was the government seemingly so uninformed on this matter? Why, if these detergents were so dangerous, did the government not act long ago? Why did the government not have its people analyze the detergents–or force the manufacturers to provide it with analytical data?

The same approach was taken when public pressure mounted to have DDT banned. The government flip-flopped and completely reversed its stand–first saying it wouldn't consider a ban and then a couple of weeks later announcing that within a year the general use of DDT would be prohibited. The mercury scare followed the same pattern. A Ph.D. student first broke the alarming news that there were relatively high levels of mercury in some species of fish. Drastic action followed, in good part because of a lack of baseline environmental studies. The most infamous of these was Ontario's "Fish for Fun" campaign, which promoted sport fishing as long as the fishermen didn't eat the fish. Some sport! Some fun!

Our generation, and perhaps the next, can still decide to impose some form of rational restraint on technology and the growth of human numbers. The time for deliberate, considered choice, however, is running out. This is especially important for the north, where restraints now will prevent costly programs of rehabilitation.

Canada, like other major countries of the world, must move to overcome these threats to our very survival. The first step should be a national policy for the environment. To be effective, this policy must be compatible and consistent with the many other needs of the country. But it also must clearly set out the intent of the people and the government of Canada to manage the environment in rational and realistic ways. And it must recognize the essence of the Trudeau Doctrine: that ecology must take precedence over economics.

A national policy for the environment should have as its goals:

1. To stop further unnecessary deterioration of the environment.
2. To restore and revitalize damaged regions.
3. To recognize that man is a part of, not apart from nature.
4. To minimize and prevent future disasters caused by uncontrolled technology.
5. To provide direction designed to optimize man-environment relationships and to minimize future costs of environmental management.

A National Environmental Policy Act should be administered by a *new* Department of the Environment which has complete authority over all actions which may affect the land, water, and air (in keeping with constitutional agreements). It is vital that while the senior bureaucrats of this department, including the deputy minister, should be noted ecologists-environmentalists, there must be a high degree of interdisciplinary cooperation and action. But we cannot leave this almost entirely in the hands of engineers and technocrats, as we do now.

The Congress of the United States passed a National Environmental Policy Act in 1969, which included in its purposes: "To declare a national policy which will encourage productive and enjoyable harmony between man and his environment; . . . to promote efforts which will prevent or eliminate damage to the environment . . . to enrich the understanding of the ecological systems and natural resources important to the Nation. . . ."[5]

One of the key features of this Act was section 102(2)(C) which required a detailed statement on every major proposal requiring federal approval and likely to have an impact on the environment. A draft report is to be prepared by the government department concerned, outlining the environmental problems, especially any adverse effects which could not be avoided if the project went ahead, and stating what can be done to minimize the effects and any alternatives. Then public hearings must be held, at which interested citizens and groups may present briefs, opinions, and criticisms. Then, according to the law, these must be evaluated and a final environmental impact statement written. Then, and only then, can a final decision be taken.

One of the first tests of this Act was the now famous Trans-Alaska Pipeline proposal. Following the discovery of oil and gas at Prudhoe Bay, Alaska, several large oil companies formed Alyeska Pipeline Service Co. to design, construct, and operate an 800-mile pipeline to transport the oil from the North Slope to Valdez, a port on the Gulf of Alaska. Plans were quickly formulated, preliminary construction began, and 48-inch pipe started to arrive from Japan.

Then, several conservation groups, who had been opposed to the pipeline from the beginning because of its potential of serious damage to the Alaskan environment, sought and obtained an injunction under Section 102 of the National Environmental Policy Act requiring the U.S. Department of the Interior to prepare an environmental impact statement before approval for the pipeline was granted. Almost two years have passed since the conservationists obtained the injunction—the impact statement has not been completed, approval has not been granted, and thousands of joints of pipe lie rusting on the tundra.

"Unfortunately," says M.P. David Anderson, chairman of the Commons Committee on Environmental Pollution, "Canadian law and administrative procedures have not been altered to permit these new environmental concerns to be adequately taken into account in public policy making."[6] There is no legislation in Canada which requires public hearings into schemes which may have profound effects on the environment. For example, a pipeline or twin lines is being proposed to bring oil and/or gas from Alaska and arctic Canada. This line would run down the Mackenzie Valley, an important waterway and wildlife area. Unlike the United States, there is no law in Canada which conservationists could turn to to fight such a project. The government has, as might be expected, issued guidelines–but we know how effective guidelines have been in the battle to contain inflation.

Anderson, an outspoken critic of government environmental policy, believes what is needed is "legislation requiring the publication of reports on which government decisions are likely to be based, and requiring public hearings on such reports prior to any decision at the Cabinet level as to whether the project should proceed."[7] The right to know is often taken for granted in a democratic country–but it is very difficult, at times even impossible, to exercise that right in Canada. I was told, for example, by Dr. John Tener, Chief of the Canadian Wildlife Service, that I could not see their files on arctic ecology because they were internal, privileged government documents. I cannot help wondering why reports on ecology should be confidential government information.

Citizens from all walks of life are becoming concerned and informed about environmental issues, in good part, perhaps, because pollution and environmental degradation touch all of us. We all breathe the same air and drink the same water. The lakes and rivers where the rich play may be as dirty as those in the crowded cities. But to be effective, citizens must show their concern in a responsible and organized manner. Unlike the United States, which has several powerful national conservation groups, such as the Sierra Club, National Audubon Society, Friends of the Earth and the Wilderness Society, there is no strong, well-organized, adequately financed association in Canada whose prime concern is the total environment.

It is a matter of utmost urgency that a viable, effective national conservation association–Environment Canada–be established. If all the Canadians who profess to be concerned about pollution, pesticides, population, and lack of parks contributed a small annual fee of, say, five dollars, we could have the kind of "think-twice" organization that is needed. It should have its headquarters in Ottawa, with regional offices across the country.

Environment Canada might have two major responsibilities –to propose ways to deal with environmental problems and to constructively criticize present policy and legislation. To be effective the association would need a large, multi-disciplinary staff capable of acting and reacting quickly. The Nader organization in the United States might be copied, especially in its use of students and recent graduates. Environment Canada is desperately needed to counter the lobbying of the mining, oil, and manufacturing interests who publicly support action to clean up the environment, but privately press for the maintenance of the status quo.

Along with a National Environmental Policy Act and a new Department of the Environment, Canada needs an Environmental Council. Such a council was recommended by a Science Council of Canada Report on Fisheries and Wildlife Research in Canada. The Environmental Quality Council, said the report, would "conduct, and publish, studies and forecasts of environmental problems in Canada, and make analytical reviews of environmental questions which are the subject of public interest. It should strive to become a major source of informed public opinion on environmental matters."[8] Such a council should, of course, be independent of political influence, similar to the Economic Council of Canada. The proposal has received the enthusiastic support of conservationists and ecologists across Canada.

There is a growing awareness, especially among the young, that we may have all the necessary technology to provide an adequate standard of living–the basic human needs, such as food, shelter, water, and clothing, are taken care of. If they are not, it is a social-political problem. The time has come when instead of continually trying to turn technology to new and

130

bigger tasks, we should attempt to iron out the imperfections in the present system. Surely we can build an automobile that does not create a menace to human health and comfort; surely we can devise a method to find oil which does not require drilling thousands of wells which may never be productive; surely we can perfect a sewage treatment process which will remove harmful chemicals before the water is returned to nature; and surely we can find means of controlling insects, which want to eat the same crops as man does, without poisoning the environment. We can—but will we?

What has this got to do with the Arctic? Perhaps everything. For there is little to be lost, but much to be gained by letting this lovely, lonely land lie fallow for a few more years. Industry, science and government are clearly not prepared to cope with this northern industrial invasion. It would be in the best interests of everyone, especially the Canadian people, if the government did call off the arctic elephant hunt. For unless there is this pause it is unlikely that the federal government will adopt a policy for the Arctic and adequately protect the environment.

"The world needs an embodiment of the frontier mythology, the sense of horizons unexplored, the mystery of uninhabited miles. It needs a place where wolves stalk the strand lines at dark because a land that can produce a wolf is a healthy, robust and perfect land." wrote Alaskan conservationist Robert Weeden.[9]

Canada's Arctic is the final frontier, the last chance on earth for man to evolve rational policies which allow "necessary economic development without unnecessary environmental destruction." The laws of the earth must become the law of the land.

NOTES TO CHAPTER 1

1. Parmenter, Bev., personal communication, April 1970.
2. *Oilweek,* May 25, 1970.
3. *Oilweek,* July 20, 1970.
4. Crombie, G. P., personal communication, May 1, 1970.
5. Warner, R. E., "Environmental Effects of Oil Pollution in Canada," report to the Canadian Wildlife Service, 1969.
6. Chrétien, J., speech to the 1971 Symposium on Petroleum Economics and Evaluation, Dallas, Texas, March 5, 1971.
7. House of Commons Debates, January 22, 1970, p. 2711.
8. Commons Standing Committee on Indian Affairs and Northern Development, Report 2, 1970.
9. *Ibid.*
10. Sproule, J. C., "Our Arctic Islands," in *Canada at Expo 70,* Japan Trade Council, 1969.
11. Lotz, J., "Notes of a Non-conference Goer," 20th Alaska Science Conference, 1969.
12. Chrétien, J., Department of Indian Affairs and Northern Development press release, October 6, 1969.
13. *Ibid.*
14. "Resolution Respecting Role of Canadian Government in Circumpolar Regions of Canada," Conference on Productivity and Conservation in Northern Lands, Oct. 15–17, 1969.
15. *Globe and Mail,* March 25, 1971.
16. Twaits, W. O., Imperial Oil Limited, Annual Report, 1969.
17. Thompson, A. R. *et al,* "Reservations re Conservation," in *Oilweek,* May 18, 1970.
18. *Globe and Mail,* May 25, 1970.
19. Hunt, A. D., *Report on Special Inspection Trip to the Mackenzie Delta Region,* May 15, 1970.
20. Department of Indian Affairs and Northern Development, communiqué, June 29, 1970.
21. Hunt, *op. cit.*
22. DIAND, see note 20.
23. Hunt, *op. cit.*
24. *Ibid.*
25. *Globe and Mail,* May 25, 1970.
26. *Ibid.*
27. Passmore, R. C., "Task Force on Northern Conservation," in *Canadian Wildlife Federation News,* Spring 1970.

28. Thompson, A. R., "Petroleum Land Policies–Alaska and Northern Canada," 1969.
29. *Ibid.*
30. *Globe and Mail,* June 20, 1970.
31. *Globe and Mail,* May 30, 1970.
32. Nickle, C. O., "Canada Revokes Crucial Reserve Order," in *Canadian Petroleum,* June 1970.
33. *Globe and Mail,* June 20, 1970.
34. Gordon, W. L., *A Choice for Canada,* Toronto, McClelland and Stewart, 1966.
35. Godfrey, J. M., quoted by Gray, E., "Tighter Control of North Oil Rights," in *Oilweek,* September 14, 1970.
36. Bill C-202, *An Act to prevent pollution of areas of the Arctic waters adjacent to the mainland and islands of the Canadian Arctic,* House of Commons, June 9, 1970.
37. Carson, Rachel, *Silent Spring,* Boston, Houghton Mifflin Co., 1962.
38. Chrétien, J., *Resource Development and Northern Ecology,* communiqué, DIAND, May 4, 1970.
39. *Ibid.*
40. Passmore, R. C., *op. cit.*

NOTES TO CHAPTER 2

1. Bliss, L. C., "Primary production within Arctic tundra ecosystems," *Proc. Conf. on Productivity and Conservation in Northern Circumpolar Lands,* 1970.
2. Porsild, A. E., "Plants in the Arctic," in *The Unbelievable Land,* Queen's Printer, 1966.
3. Tuck, L. M., *The Murres,* Canadian Wildlife Service, 1961.
4. Clarke, C. H. D., *A Biological Investigation of the Thelon Game Sanctuary,* National Museum of Canada, Bulletin 96, 1940.
5. Dunbar, M. J., *Ecological Development in Polar Regions,* Englewood Cliffs, N.J., Prentice-Hall, 1968.

NOTES TO CHAPTER 3

1. United Nations Educational and Social Council, *Conservation and Rational Use of the Biosphere,* Document E/4458, 1968.
2. Bliss, L. C. *High Arctic Tundra IBP Proposal,* (mimeo), 1969.
3. *Ibid.*

4. Chrétien, Jean, "Resource Development and Northern Ecology," speech to Canadian Transportation Research Forum, 1970.
5. *Ibid.*
6. Dunbar, M. J., *Ecological Development in Polar Regions,* Englewood Cliffs, N.J., Prentice-Hall, 1968.
7. Canadian Wildlife Service, *How to Use the Arctic Ecology Map Series,* (mimeo), 1971.
8. *Ibid.*
9. "Recommendations of the Biosphere Conference," in *Biological Conservation,* Vol. 1, No. 3, 1969.
10. Ewing, M. and Donn, W. L., "Pleistocene Climate Changes," in *Geology of the Arctic,* Toronto, University of Toronto Press, 1961, Vol. 2.

NOTES TO CHAPTER 4

1. Schofield, E. and Hamilton, W. L., *Probable Damage to Arctic Ecosystems through Air-pollution Effects on Lichens,* Ohio State University, Institute of Polar Studies.
2. *Ibid.*
3. Macpherson, A. H., "The Oil Rush and the Arctic Environment," manuscript.
4. Brief prepared for the Canadian Wildlife Service, August 14, 1969.
5. Pruitt, W., "Permafrost and its Significance for Biological Communities," paper presented at Conference on Productivity and Conservation in Northern Circumpolar Lands, Oct. 1969.
6. Lachenbruch, A. H., *Some Estimates of the Thermal Effects of a Heated Pipeline in Permafrost,* Washington, U.S. Government Printing Office, Geological Survey Circular 632.
7. Quoted in *News of the North,* Aug. 20, 1970.
8. Watmore, T. G., "Arctic Oil Play Facing Thermal Erosion Problems in Permafrost Environments," in *Canadian Petroleum,* March 1969, pp. 10-14.
9. Naysmith, J. K., "Conservation in Canada's North," paper presented at Conference on Productivity and Conservation in Northern Circumpolar Lands, October 1969.
10. Statement at Conference on Productivity and Conservation in Northern Circumpolar Lands, October 1969.
11. McTaggart Cowan, Ian, "Ecology and Northern Development," in *Arctic,* 22:1, March 1969, pp. 1-11.
12. House of Commons Debates, 114:78, March 3, 1970, p. 4313.
13. Fuller, W. A., "Environmental Quality in the Mid North," manuscript.
14. *Ibid.*
15. See McTaggart Cowan, *op. cit.*
16. Pimlott, D. H. *et al,* "Fisheries and Wildlife Research in Canada," Science Council of Canada, to be published 1971.
17. McTaggart Cowan, *op. cit.*
18. House of Commons Debates, 114:57, February 2, 1970, p. 3102.

NOTES TO CHAPTER 5

1. Pimlott, D. H., "Wilderness in Canada," in *The Living Wilderness,* vol. 32, no. 103, 1968.
2. The National Parks Act, Ottawa, Queen's Printer.
3. Brooks, L., and Eidsvick, H., *National Park Potentials: Northwest Territories and Yukon,* National Parks Branch, Report 63-3, 1963.
4. National and Provincial Parks Association of Canada, resolution re Great Slave National Park, May 27, 1966.
5. Northwest Territories Chamber of Mines position re park proposal, presented by Norman W. Byme, President, N.W.T. Chamber of Mines, June 24, 1969.
6. *Ibid.*
7. *Ibid.*
8. *New York Times,* August 15, 1971.
9. *Ibid.*
10. Leopold, Luna B., "Landscape Esthetics," in *Natural History,* October 1968.
11. Quoted in *Toronto Telegram,* February 28, 1970.
12. Hemstock, R. A., "Industry and the Arctic Environment," speech to the Royal Society of Canada, June 3, 1970.

NOTES TO CHAPTER 6

1. Quoted in *News of the North,* January 22, 1970.
2. Minutes of a meeting of the Privy Council, June 25, 1959.
3. Pearson, Roger, "Resource Management Strategies and Area Viability,"

Ph.D. thesis, University of Illinois, 1969.

4. The Fitz-Smith Band and Tebacha Association, brief to the Government of Canada, July 1968.

5. Department of Indian Affairs and Northern Development, *Indian Policy: politique indienne,* 1969.

6. Quoted in *News of the North,* March 12, 1970.

7. *Ibid.*

8. Jenness, Diamond, "Eskimo Administration: II, Canada," Arctic Institute of North America, Technical Paper No. 14, 1964.

9. From transcript of the Prime Minister's remarks at the Vancouver Liberal Association Dinner, Seaforth Armories, Vancouver, B.C., August 8, 1969.

10. Simonie, Michael, Council of the Northwest Territories Debates, 41st Session, January 14, 1970, p. 101.

11. *Globe and Mail,* August 1, 1970.

12. Resolution No. 1, Arctic Native Conference, Coppermine, N.W.T., quoted in *TAWPE,* Aug. 3, 1970.

13. *Globe and Mail,* October 13, 1970,

14. Department of Indian Affairs and Northern Development, *Accord Reached on Banks Island Oil and Gas Exploration,* Communiqué 1-7083, October 2, 1970.

15. Chrétien, Jean, letter to the editor, *Globe and Mail,* October 13, 1970.

16. *Ibid.*

17. *An Act for the Recognition and Protection of Human Rights and Fundamental Freedoms,* 8-9 Elizabeth II, Chap. 44, August 10, 1970.

18. Quoted in Trudeau, P. E., *A Canadian Charter of Human Rights,* Queen's Printer, 1968.

19. *News of the North,* October 8, 1970.

20. COPE, By-laws, Inuvik, 1970.

21. Personal interview, Yellowknife, N.W.T., February 17, 1970.

22. Goldberg, Arthur J., on Alaska Native Land Claims, Hearing before the Committee on Interior and Insular Affairs, S. 1830, April 29, 1969, p. 87.

23. Cumming, Peter A., *loc. cit.*

NOTES TO CHAPTER 7

1. House of Commons Debates, Oct. 24, 1969, p. 39.

2. Transcript of Prime Minister's remarks on CBC TV, April 19, 1970.

3. Bill C-202, An Act to prevent pollution of areas of the arctic waters adjacent to the mainland and islands of the Canadian Arctic, Ottawa, House of Commons, June 9, 1970.

4. Quoted in Cahn, Robert, *Ecology and International Assistance,* Washington, D.C., The Conservation Foundation, 1968.

5. Transcript of Prime Minister's remarks on CTV, May 12, 1970.

6. "General Assembly Adopts Resolution on 1972 World Conference on the Human Environment," United Nations Office of Public Information, Background Note No. 161, December 24, 1969.

7. Jenness, Diamond, *Eskimo Administration: Analysis and Reflections,* Arctic Institute of North America, Technical Paper No. 21, March 1968.

8. House of Commons Debates, October 24, 1969, p. 39.

9. Transcript of Prime Minister's remarks on CTV, May 12, 1970.

NOTES TO CHAPTER 8

1. Thompson, A. R., "A Conservation Regime for the North–What Have Lawyers to Offer?," paper presented at Conference on Productivity and Conservation in Northern Circumpolar Lands, Edmonton, Alberta, October 1969.

2. Cutler, M., "Canada will continue to press for an open U.S. oil market", *Oilweek,* Vol. 21, No. 4, 1969, p. 29.

3. Tour–Panarctic Oil's Operations in Canada's Far North, arranged by Department of Indian Affairs and Northern Development, August 17-19, 1968.

4. Toronto, Ryerson Press/Maclean-Hunter, 1969.

5. McClements, Robert, Jr., "The Athabasca Tar Sands", in *Dusters and Gushers,* Toronto, Pitt Publishing Co., 1968.

6. Ottawa, National Energy Board, 1969.

7. Lotz, J., "The Myth of the Rich North," in *Canadian Forum,* January 1968.

8. Twaits, W. O., "Oil and Capital–1970," paper presented at Annual Meeting of the Canadian Life Insurance Association, Investment Section, Toronto, May 12, 1970.

9. Jenness, Diamond, *Eskimo Administration: Analysis and Reflections,*

Arctic Institute of North America, Technical Paper No. 21, March 1968.

10. *Canada North of 60: an introduction to resource and economic development in the Yukon and the Northwest Territories,* pamphlet, Department of Indian Affairs and Northern Development.

11. Passmore, R. C., "Crisis in the North," Canadian Wildlife Federation News Release, February 1970.

12. *Bulletin of the Conservation Council of Ontario,* April 1970, p. 16.

13. Fuller, W. A., "Ecological Impact of Arctic Development", 20th Alaska Science Conference, University of Alaska, College, Alaska, Aug. 24-27, 1969.

14. Published by W. H. Freeman and Co., San Francisco, Cal.

15. Passmore, R. C., *op cit.*

16. Chrétien, J., in "Canada North of 60 . . ." (see note 10).

17. "The Waiting Wealth," Toronto, Playfair and Co.

18. Fraser, Blair, *The Search for Identity,* Toronto, Doubleday, 1967.

19. Clarke, C. H. D., *A Biological Investigation of the Thelon Game Sanctuary,* National Museum of Canada, Bulletin No. 96, 1940.

20. Debates of the Senate, Vol. 117, No. 95, Oct. 14, 1969, pp. 1826-29.

21. "The Biosphere Conference: Final Report," Document SC/MD/9, Paris, UNESCO, January 1969.

22. Transcript of Prime Minister's remarks to the Annual Meeting of the Canadian Press, Toronto, April 15, 1970.

23. Twaits, W. O., report to the shareholders, in Imperial Oil Limited Annual Report, 1969, pp. 1-24.

24. Quoted in the *Globe and Mail,* August 4, 1970.

25. Nichol, Senator John, *op. cit.*

NOTES TO CHAPTER 9

1. Galbraith, J. K., *The New Industrial State,* Houghton Mifflin Co., 1967.

2. Scott, R. F., "Effects of Ecology on Technical Change," *Proc. Alaska Science Conference,* No. 20, 1969.

3. Commoner, Barry, *Science and Survival,* Viking Press, 1966.

4. Dasmann, R. F., *The U.S. Environment: a Time to Decide,* Population Reference Bureau Publication No. 25, 1968.

5. Congress of the United States, National Environmental Policy Act, 1969.

6. Anderson, David, "Your Environment and You," in *Wildlife News,* Vol. 7, Nos. 2 & 3, 1971.

7. *Ibid.*

8. Science Council of Canada, Report on Fisheries and Wildlife Research in Canada, Report No. 9, 1970.

9. Weeden, Robert, "Man in Nature: a Strategy for Alaskan Living," *Proc. Conference on Productivity and Conservation in Northern Circumpolar Lands,* IUCN, No. 16, 1970.

Bibliography

Baird, Patrick D. *The Polar World,* London: Longmans, 1964.

Cooley, Richard. *Alaska: A Challenge in Conservation,* Madison: University of Wisconsin Press, 1966.

Dunbar, M. J. *Ecological Development in Polar Regions,* Toronto: Prentice-Hall, 1968.

Fuller, W. A. and Kevan, P. G., eds. *Productivity and Conservation in Northern Circumpolar Lands,* Morges: International Union for the Conservation of Nature, 1970.

Godfrey, W. E. *The Birds of Canada,* Ottawa: Queen's Printer, 1966.

Gray, Earle. *Impact of Oil,* Toronto: Ryerson Press/Maclean Hunter, 1969.

Jenness, Diamond. *Eskimo Administration: II Canada,* Montreal: Arctic Institute of North America, 1964.

Kelsall, J. P. *The Caribou,* Ottawa: Queen's Printer, 1968.

Lotz, J. *Northern Realities,* Toronto: New Press, 1970.

Macdonald, R. St. J., ed. *The Arctic Frontier,* University of Toronto Press, 1966.

Polunin, Nicholas. *Circumpolar Arctic Flora,* Oxford University Press, 1959.

Porsild, A. E. *Illustrated Flora of the Canadian Arctic Archipelago,* Ottawa: Queen's Printer, 1964.

Pruitt, W. *Animals of the North,* New York: Harper and Row, 1967.

Raasch, G. O., ed. *Geology of the Arctic,* University of Toronto Press, 1961 (2 vols.).

Rea, K. J. *The Political Economy of the Canadian North,* University of Toronto Press, 1968.

Rohmer, Richard. *The Green North: Mid Canada,* Toronto: Maclean-Hunter, 1970.

Seton, E. T. *The Arctic Prairies,* New York: Scribner's, 1912.

Smith, Norman I., ed. *The Unbelievable Land,* Ottawa: Queen's Printer, 1964.

Steensel, M. van, ed. *People of Light and Dark,* Ottawa: Queen's Printer, 1966.

Symington, F. *Tuktu,* Ottawa: Queen's Printer, 1965.

Tener, J. S. *Muskoxen in Canada,* Ottawa: Queen's Printer, 1965.

Wilkinson, Douglas. *The Arctic Coast,* Toronto: Natural Science Library of Canada, 1970.